Staying Motivated: Why They Sell and How They Stay Motivated

First Edition

ISBN: 978-1-300-19505-4

I0390432

Category: Business

Description: If you watched the news on just about any day of the week, you will agree there has never been a bigger need for highly motivated professional sales people. When prices skyrocket, the stock market tumbles, and customers are worried, it's time for you, the person on the front line of the economy, to jump in, attack, and truly make a difference. Costs are going up on every front. The price of gas, hotel rooms, airline tickets and the cost of a meal are just a few things that have a direct effect on you. You will HAVE to raise your prices and at the same time make your customer feel good about paying more!

Keywords: sales motivation, staying motivated, motivating sales people, career in sales, sales training, sales instruction, sales techniques, improved sales

Author: Bob Oros, www.BobOros.com

ISBN 978-1-300-19505-4
90000

9 781300 195054

WHY THEY SELL AND HOW THEY STAY MOTIVATED .1

4

5

SECTION 2 STAYING MOTIVATED 110

If you watched the news on just about any day of the week, you will agree there has never been a bigger need for professional sales people. When prices skyrocket, the stock market tumbles, and customers are worried, it's time for you, the person on the front line of the economy, to jump in, attack, and truly make a difference.

Your costs are going up on every front. The price of gas, hotel rooms, airline tickets and the cost of a meal are just a few things that have a direct effect on you. You will HAVE to raise your prices and at the same time make your customer feel good about paying more! To the average person, that sounds like an impossible mission! But for the professional sales person, it's what we do.

If you have ever wondered what goes on in the mind of a sales person, how they remain positive in the face of gloom and doom, your curiosity can now be satisfied. Some of the best sales professionals share their thoughts about why they chose a sales career and how they keep themselves motivated.

Section 1 Why Sales...

People who have never felt the pain of defeat and agony of rejection, never been turned down over and over again yet kept on going, never lived out of a suit case for weeks at a time traveling from airport to airport, dealing with overcrowded airplanes, navigating rental cars in strange cities, calling on pressured and short-tempered buyers and purchasing agents, up late wining and dining, only to leave the next morning on the 6:00 am flight to do it all over again wonder WHY WE DO IT AND LOVE EVERY MINUTE OF IT! People simply don't understand. That's why this collection of comments was compiled – for YOU – SOMEONE ALREADY IN SALES OR CONSIDERING A CAREER IN SALES.

In response to the following challenge, I received the replies in this book from my friends and colleagues with **sound advice about a career in sales**...

Here it is... You are standing before 1,000 potential salespeople and you have been chosen as the ambassador of a sales career. You have to give a speech on this topic:

WHY I BELIEVE A CAREER IN SALES
IS THE BEST JOB IN THE WORLD

01 Chuck Mastruserio, Regional Manager Ember Farms

What makes sales the best job in the world? For me its not one single thing it's a collection of things. Having grown into this job of sales in the meat business for over 25 years I have accumulated knowledge from the different positions I have held. I find that being able to consult with prospects and help them by educating them from my real life experience very rewarding. This is another part of my position that I particularly like. As a result of this support I find that I have made a new friend. Only *this* friend pays your commission and isn't borrowing it!

Overall though, the sales occupation isn't rocket science, but there are a lot of formulas that make you a successful sales person. The very basics I have found to be are this. 1) Enjoy the product you are selling. 2) Do what you say you are going to do for a customer or prospect before you say you re going to do it. 3) Follow up promptly. 4) Be honest.

02 Thax Turner, Sales Professional

I hope your doing great! Why I believe sales is the best job in the world? You know life isn't about finding yourself. Life is about creating yourself! In sales you get to create yourself daily. Everyday is a new day with opportunity. You get to put a need with a solution to fulfill your day!!!

03 Scott Yelle, VP Sales, Sysco San Francisco

It's the greatest job in the world because you are able to help people succeed in their business, because you have the freedom and flexibility to create your own schedule, because you have unlimited earning potential, because as you develop great relationships with your customers, they become friends. Wouldn't trade it for the world!

04 Ray Nicholas, Sysco Division President

I sold meat for my brother for my first year with Newport Meat Co. down South. It was the best of times; it was the worst of times. Gulf war started, gas rationing, you name it, but the reasons I started in sales still holds true for many who have remained in the profession.

1. For many sales positions, unlimited income potential. The more you sell the more you make. Obviously this would apply to commission type positions.

2. Extreme levels of freedom. You can usually set your work hours. Extended lunches leave early start late. If you are successful, you have lots of additional freedoms that are not associated with an office environment.

3. Lots of independence. No boss looking over your shoulder.
4. Sharing the Entrepreneurial spirit, with out the investment of a business. You can make and do what you choose as long as you are bringing in the "bacon".

05 Michael Kelly, Sales Professional, Feesers Foodservice, Inc.

I would be glad to give you a couple of ideas... you have helped me without question!

I have 2 1/2 years of food sales experience, in other words, I am a rookie. I believe that Sales is the best job in the world for me for the following reasons:

I truly enjoy working with people and helping them make decisions on buying. Successful selling is proportionate to the relationship that you have with your customers. I cannot pick who I want as a customer, I have to make the sale to all that will buy. Periodic reviews will later decide which customers are truly worth my time.

I was a chef for 20 years which has really helped me in my food sales career. You have to really know what you are selling and then be passionate about selling it. I think it would be difficult to switch from selling cars to selling food.

I love the fact that I'm on the move each day going where I want instead of sitting all day at a desk job.

Only I decide when I will get a raise. If I spend time on planning each day, I will produce sales which not only increases my pay, but gives me the benefits (trips...) that I was working so hard for. An expression from my Father; Sales is like shaving- if you don't do it everyday, you're a bum!

Understand that each industry changes at some point, and new approaches to selling are needed. Learn how to adjust to these changes through a course like Bob's. It is really helping me! Thanks again Bob for all of your help!

06 Dr. Burt Smith, CEO Executive Marketing Information

My response is, because if you know how to sell, you will ALWAYS be employed! This is the ONLY profession with job security! Selling is the most important aspect of business because it contributes to the TOP LINE. Without a top line, there is no bottom line! If sales people stopped performing, our economy would come to a grinding halt because consumption drives our economy! Zig Ziglar once also aptly pointed out that there are more salespeople who are millionaires than doctors!

07 Anthony Moorhead, Pittsburgh Seafood

1. The workday will NEVER be the same as the day before.

2. You will face new exciting challenges ever day.

3. Independence and self gratification.

4. You can determine your own income and give yourself your own raises

08 Gerald "Chip" McFall, District Manager, US Food Service, KY

I believe that sales is the greatest profession in the world because every great leader started with the sale. He is responsible for convincing his followers the path in which to choose, the product in which to buy, the idea in which to invest. Jesus persuaded 12, which lead to billions of sales that followed and a better way of life for billions of people. All the great prophets, business owners, inventors started out persuading a group of people on an idea. Sales and persuasion are the spark that starts every great ventures.

In business nothing starts until the first case is sold. No manufacture makes the case, no distributor buys the case, no driver delivers the case, no warehousemen picks the case, no customer resells the case. None of these people receives a paycheck each week until someone persuades another on an idea. The paycheck that keeps the lights on and their children feed.

It all starts with the person brave enough, persistent enough and determined enough to make the first sale.

09 Michael A. Farha, Sales Professional, Ben E. Keith Foods

Why I believe that a career in sales the best job in the world. There are some many wonderful things about being in sales. Every day is a brand new adventure, a new place and new faces. You get the opportunity to work on your own with an incredible amount of freedom and creativity. You are out amongst the people helping them solve their problems by presenting solutions. The chance to compete head to head in a job that absolutely rewards a smart, strong work ethic. You will be paid on job performance.

10 Phil Williams, Sales Professional

College seniors need to understand that whether they are aware of it or not, every man, woman and child alive is in the sales profession. Our lives are consumed every day attempting to sell something to someone in our lives. It may be tangible goods, services, or ideology, but we are constantly striving to sell something in our lives even if we don't think of it as sales. That said, embrace the concept; over come your innate fears of sales; learn and practice the fundamentals of professional sales; and enjoy a rewarding life!

11 Matt Browning, Territory Manager, U.S. Foodservice

There are several reasons why sales is the best job in the world. Especially food sales. I have a passion for food and I get to interact with food and food people everyday. I love the fact that I determine my own income. When I was in the restaurant I worked seventy hour weeks and months at a time without a day off. I gave myself to my job and I knew exactly what I was bringing home each week. Now I get rewarded proportionately for my work. Before I could have sat in my office with my feet up, five days a week, clocked out after 8 hours and made the same amount of money. That's not me though.

 I love the fact that if I do my job right all of my customer's lives get better. They make more money, have more time, are happier. None of that is what gets me going in the morning. I love to win. I want to be the best. I want to be better than all my competitors. I want to be better than all my coworkers. I want a guy that's been in the restaurant business his whole life to say that's the best sales rep I have ever had. I want to be better than I was yesterday, last week and last year. I hate when I walk out of a customer or a prospect and I didn't win every single piece of business in there. Sales is the best job in the world because I have a daily quantifiable ability to be the best.

12 Tom Wheat, President, Cable Meat Center, Inc

"Nothing happens until something is sold." The best product, the best manufacturing facility, the latest technology, the most qualified work force, or all the capital you might possible need – all are standing idle until something is sold.

Sales is the driving force behind commerce. It is an exciting, dynamic, challenging, and at the same time a very difficult task. You are only limited by yourself. The sky is the limit to personal achievement and financial success. Helping customers solve problems and meet their goals builds unique relationships.

I own my own small food distributorship. Only about 30% of my time can be devoted to sales. I wish that percentage was more like 70%.

13 Gary Sells, Sales Professional, Ginsberg's Foods

Sales allows you the independence of becoming as rich as you want to. It allows you to be a self starter. It allows you to be an independent part of a team. It allows you to manage yourself. It allows you to be confident in your OWN abilities. It allows you to sell to whomever YOU want to... It gives you personal freedom and accountability to a team. Sales IS the best job YOU can have......provided YOU want to succeed!!

14 Bernard Rigal, Sales Professional, San Jose, CA

My comments for new people that would like to be in sales is to believe and like what they sell and be able to show others why you should buy from them. I always think of the rule that I learn from another great speaker like you - people buy from people and the 3 PPP are:

People ~~ Product ~~ Profit

My other comment is that you are in control of your time and you can make a lot of money for yourself. In many cases the sales people are making way more than their branch president.

15 Corry Givens, Sales Professional, Banta Foods

Thanks for the opportunity to be included in this special report. What I believe is that sales is the BEST JOB IN THE WORLD for the RIGHT PERSON. Sales is NOT for everyone, but is the easiest job to get into. But for a person who can stay POSITIVE and have the ability to SELL THEMSELVES and APPLY WHAT YOU KNOW and have THREE YEARS to feel confident and be able see OPPORTUNITIES and be able to DO WHAT YOU SAY YOU'LL DO and be able to BUILD TRUST with your customers as well as SEPARATE YOURSELF FROM COMPETITION and be able to PUT CUSTOMERS FIRST and show customer you APPRECIATE THEIR BUSINESS and be able to CAREFULLY LISTEN and let the customer know that you are SINCERELY INTERESTED IN HELPING THEM. Be able to handle REJECTION. Be a GOAL SETTER as well as a DO IT NOW ATTITUDE and finally be able RELIVE AND BUILD ON THEIR ACHIEMENT AND SUCCESS RESULTING IN HIGHER AND HIGHER EXPECTATION. Then sales IS the best job in the world, but for a person who can not achieve this - they are just another statistic.

16 Scott Nicotra, Territory Manager, US Foodservice

The reason why we have the greatest job in the world is because day in and day out, we get to help someone! To me that's what helps me roll out of bed in the morning... I always approach everyone with the "How can I help you today" attitude! Just knowing you have given someone an alternative in life speaks more than money!!

17 Amy Grimm, Sales Professional, Performance Food Group

My first thought when I read this...when in front of a group of salespeople and you ask the question how many of you always wanted to be a salesperson when you were growing up? Then narrow it down by asking how many of thought you would be selling (groceries, insurance, cars, roofs, landscaping, etc.) A sales position requires much self discipline but also allows for a flexible schedule. A sales position allows one to be in control of his or her paycheck. A sales position requires the ability to accept rejection. I once had someone tell me his daily goal was to be told "No, not interested 10 times a day."

18 Cori Mazzotta, Regional Sales Manger, Ember Farms

I believe a job in sales is the best job in the world because you are meeting and developing relationships with new people everyday. You are helping people by filling their needs with the product or service you sell. Depending on the sales job you have, you may get to see the country or even the world. Lastly because of all of the above I feel that sales is the best job in the world because it does not feel like a job, it is fun.

19 Trip English, Sales Professional, Ben E. Keith Foods

There are shows like "ER", "Boston Legal", "Monday Night Football", "24", "Jag" and a host of other dramas or reality shows that glorify great professions that you may be interested in.

Why would you want to get in sales? How do you get in sales? Is there an MBA out there available for "sales"?

Actually you have been in sales before; you just did not know it.

Did you sell lemonade as a kid? That is sales.

Did you ever ask for something and you got it? That is sales. (You negotiated)

Did you ever work at a golf course? That is sales.

Did you ever work in fast food, a restaurant, a shoe store, anywhere at the mall?

Did you ever buy bulk candy and take it to school to sell? I did, and I made a killing.

Sales is something you like to do. You like to describe a product, talk about the features and benefits, and ask for the sale.

When your customer says "sure, I will buy one" you light up.

You *did* sell it. This is not something that the customer picked out of a vending machine. You made the presentation and made the sale. You made the commission of the sale. You made it happen.

20 Frank Barcelona, Regional Sales Manager, Ember Farms

Why sales is the best career in the world for me is

Personal satisfaction after delivering results

Ability to earn a good living to help support your family.

21 Diane R.Vieira, Regional Manager, Northeast, Ember Farms

I BELIEVE THAT A CAREER IN SALES IS THE BEST JOB IN THE WORLD:

 - I am a major factor in my own fulfilled Goals and Accomplishments.

- I am continually in the process of learning and training.

- I have the Independence and satisfaction in the balancing of my Professional Career and my Family.

 Most importantly, My Career in Sales has lead me to meet the most dynamic, strong character and honest group of people. There are also those I have me that I believe do not meet this high standard. My persistence, ability and character are challenged. These challenges are the times that I am able to reflect on who I am, to realize the dignity and differences of all people and most importantly the fact that a career in sales can bring you to a place of great satisfaction.

22 Wayne Gauldin, Pocahontas Foods (Retired)

Being a DSR is a very rewarding job and it is ONE where, as they say, you CAN write your own ticket.

In order for the job to be loved...loved enough to want no other job...then the person must really commit to the job.

I knew a DSR earning 115,000 a year in 1980. Not bad. And there were many others. If you spend the time to do the homework, learn the computer skills, and HAVE A SENSE OF URGENCY............customers will flock to you.

My wife Betty is a DSR. She works 80 hours and loves every minute of it. Handling 40 accounts spread out over 4 counties, her customers are like family. The personal interaction in which they see HER as knowing all about their business has been and continues to be the key to her success. It's almost like she "manages" 40 businesses and goes beyond to assure THEIR success.   The reward is more than monetary.

23 Amy Fitzpatrick, Sales and Marketing-H.C. Brill Company

I have been thinking about your question and having been in direct sales and now being in the corporate office with my company I can fully appreciate field sales (and can't wait to get back to the field!).

Here is what I remember when I graduated as a Wildlife Biologist and I think all college kids regardless of their major feel upon graduation: You have worked hard for at least 4 years, you are ambitious and the world is your oyster. You have all the abilities to change the world!

Sales is the only career that I have found that to be true. Your reward and success are truly based on the effort and drive you put forth. It may take a little time but it will happen and you can change world whether it be with your product or the relationships you build in helping your customer build their business. At Brill, our philosophy is that we become successful as you (the customer) become successful.

Sales are one area which you are truly in control of your ultimate destiny. You are unhampered with time schedules set by others so your time is your own to utilize to the utmost efficiency. Your motivation is set by you and your peers. Most outcomes are a product of YOUR choice. Not many more careers can offer that.

24 Jeff Ramesbottom, Territory Manager/US Foodservice

If I had to answer that question, I would tell the folks that selling is the best career because everyday is a new and exciting challenge. The satisfaction you receive from helping people find solutions to their business problems is unparalleled. In addition, what other job provides you with unlimited earning capacity.

25 Chesley Wyatt, Director of Training, Ben E Keith Foods

There is no better job in the world then being in sales and the reasons are simple. A person that is disciplined in their goal setting and expects and wants more this profession provides that. The only competition one has in sales is themselves and when this is realized we only become better.

26 Terry Miller, Sales Representative, Mid-America Wholesale

This intrigues me because I have often wondered how I ended up in a job I truly love. I love the competition involved in sales just as I love sports. You can compete to the death but keep it clean and shake hands afterwards with your rival if you play fair. The ability to out work out hustle out think and out do your job all depends on yourself.

Being your own boss but not having to run a business and worry about all the finer points like payroll and inventory and taxes and repairs, etc.

Sales just can't be beat. The paydays are nice too.

27 Tammy Hand, Staffing Coordinator

I believe being in sales is the best job in the world. It has so many advantages.

Being in sales is like owning your own company. There is so much room for growth with each new day. Every morning is like a new adventure into the world unknown.

You have a wonderful opportunity to meet new people, form positive relationships and make money all at the same time.

Being able to set your own schedule and goals is only a few advantages to mention.

There are always obstacles with every job, no matter what field you're in, but with sales you can use your own strategy and go at your own speed to conquer every obstacle there is.

Once someone really sees how great sales is, it's hard to convince them there's any other line of work out there.

Having and keeping a positive attitude about sales will only help you succeed in an employment that's already awesome.

28 Kenny Siegel, Sales Manager, Swiss Chalet Fine Foods

It was scary for me to think about a sales career in the beginning. I didn't understand anything about sales. All I thought about was the reputation of car salesmen. Then I realized someone is going to buy something from someone so it may as well be from me!

I believe working in sales is the greatest career ever. It is more than just a job. It forces you to improve yourself in all areas of your life. The challenge and the opportunities are rewarding financially and monetarily. I have the freedom to set my schedule as well as my income. The more I sell the more money I earn! What a concept!

When people ask what I do to earn a living I tell them I am in the people business. I love sales and I love people, after all they are my species, what a perfect fit. After 24 years in sales I have never looked back. I am excited everyday to make new friends and make money helping them. If you are thinking about a job sales may not be for you. If you are thinking about a professional career than sales is a perfect avenue!

29 Jonathan Gifford, Sales Manager

Why I believe a career in sales is the best job in the world:

For me I never really knew what I wanted to be growing up. It took me 4yrs in college (getting a degree that has nothing to do with what I do now) 4 years in the army and then it hit me I have a personality that I think will help me succeed in one area and luckily a very broad area SALES. I am in a particular field, food service and I love it but the truth is sales is sales and I know I can sell anything from asparagus to Xerox printer (that whole y-z thing not real good at selling them). The truth is the fact that I have a challenge every day sales is not easy and every morning when I wake up I am excited about getting out there and pushing myself into areas I have never been.

When prospecting no two operators are the same they all have different bents to certain things. With that said no two sales are made the same I can close a sale with this guy real easy but down the road there may be a guy with the exact same need but he is a little harder.

Challenge - that's what it is all about. I also really like the fact I do not have a sales manager breathing down my back (of course I am the sales manager now) when I was on the street I looked at it as my own business minus all the over head, legal fees, employees, etc.... You have the best of both worlds. I never had an issue with taking off on a Wednesday afternoon around three to go home and play with my son. I knew I had everything done before that and the truth is I would work twice as hard to get the cold calls in on those days. (as a sales manager I still have no issue with that if I know my DSR's are doing what is right) Being in sales is a great freedom others just do not have. So the challenge, the natural ability to talk to any one about anything (no one has a natural ability to sell), and the freedom I have are the main reasons I have chosen to be in sales.

30 Terry R. Barr, Category Manager, Brown Food Service

I have worked in sales for over 35 years and have never regretted it. Where else can you give yourself a raise just by making an extra call a day? Where else do you get the satisfaction of helping someone with a need that fits their desires and makes them happy? Of course it is stressful, of course you have goals to meet and quotas to meet, but if you are organized, love your work and have product knowledge the stress level is greatly reduced. Selling something is serious work, you are providing a service or product to someone to fit their needs and wants and you must to make sure that they are happy and refer your service when they are done and that the product or service does it's job. Have I had my good days and bad days, yes, but so does everyone else, but as a sales person, consultant or whatever you call yourself, we have freedom. Do I love what I have been doing all these years, I love it, and can you imagine, they actually pay me to do it. Sales is the best, we are no longer the peddlers of old, we are consultants and problem solvers. Quite a daunting task and when the customer says "thanks", you feel good inside and know you did a "job well done".

31 Mike Melton, Sales Manager

The sky is the limit. A career in sales will allow you to build and hone creativity and establish expertise, independence and individuality. A career in sales will also allow you to build your own future while helping others with theirs along the way.

32 Steve Benyo, President & CEO, Pittsburgh Seafood's

Bob, how can I stand up in front of all those impressionable young minds of potential sales people...and lie to them? A sales career is actually the second best career in the world. Those of us who are "in the know" may be keeping our big secret very hush-hush, but sooner or later, the truth will leak out: The World's Best Career is _being Bob Oros_.....the world-class sales trainer! From up on that perch, everything else probably appears tiny.

33 Ken Cone, President & CEO, Cone Financial

Bob the best thing about being a sales person is that they are normally the highest paid employees next to the owner of any company, they are normally free thinker's, and they are problem solvers. Sales people also have the most flexible work hours of any employee.

34 Mike Rohan, Sales Professional

I think a career in sales is the best job in the world because:

1) Everyone--including prospects for my service--needs help with something.

2) Its a detective story--you have to solve a problem with the clues you have or the questions you ask.

3) If a prospect doesn't need what I offer today, they may need it tomorrow.

4) People are more interesting than inanimate objectives in other work.

5) Every day offers something new--I'm never bored.

6) Success is only up to me--no one else.

35 Anthony Paventi, Sales Training Manager, US Foodservice

The question, "Why do you want a career in sales" is the last question I ask in my interviews. "This is why everyone should want a career in sales" is a module I teach during training.

Here are the responses/material:

It's your own business
- You are your own boss
- You have unlimited potential
- Flexible hours
- Advancement in the company, (DSM, RSM, VP's)
- You learn something new every day
- Every day is different
- You are not stuck in an office every day
- The Relationships you build
- With the right company, you are trained to succeed
- You get to be the hero (problem solving, customer needs)

36 Paul Nottingham, Training Manager, Food Services of America

I could write a speech for many of the different things that make a sales career a great one. I will list some bullet points

~~Give yourself the raise you deserve EVERY DAY!!!!

~~Create partnerships in business that will provide ever growing opportunities to succeed, and Prosper.

~~The ability to learn from the BEST how to become the BEST and BETTER!

~~Daily challenges that elevate your interpersonal and problem solving skills to a new level.

~~Provide the intangible service that provides tangible results!

~~Develop skill sets that never go out of demand.

~~Become a lifelong student of Interpersonal relationships, Business in general and Service as a profession.

~~Realize the true meaning of why God gave you Two ears and one mouth.

~~To appreciate that Loyalty can't be purchased-it must be earned.

~~To realize the thrill of victory and the agony defeat, many times in the same day!!

~~To challenge your own integrity and win- over and over again.

~~To silently understand the Need behind the need and smile, while your competition never gets it.

~~To be acknowledged for the value you create by the most important people in the world-YOUR CUSTOMERS!

~~To be a business partner in dozens of businesses all at the same time.

~~To become the master of your time management and create opportunities for better quality of life.

~~To allow yourself to become a trusted member of the customers "Family" and held accountable as such.

~~To be thought of first when the really big things need fixing, and to be thought of first when the little things happen too.

~~To hear the words" Paul takes care of me and while your prices might be better today, He is consistent everyday!

~~To feel a level of pride just by seeing one of your delivery trucks or a Sugar packet in your favorite restaurant!

~~To know the Effort was worth it when your spouse joins you on the trip you won in the contest-AGAIN!

~~To see a big part of your income that is not in an hourly wage or weekly salary, and know you decide what it will be

~~To have People like Bob Oros a true professional seek your opinion, because he understands the Blood, sweat and tears you pour into this profession, and he salutes you just as much as you admire him!

37 Dominick Yarnal, Sales Professional

Why I Believe Sales is the Best Job in the World

Sales is one of those unique jobs. I get to travel. I get to meet different people everyday. Sales can be very challenging, as well as rewarding. Everyday is a new adventure. When dealing with different people, I get to see that we are all different from character to temperaments, and some of these traits can change more than once from the beginning of the sale to the end. Everyday is a new challenge because, if trying to please different individuals isn't difficult enough, you also have to deal with delivery times, out of stocks and substitutions. By the end of the day, or sale, there is a certain sense of accomplishment knowing you did all you could to please on average 20-25 different dispositions. Some you win, some you lose, but you go back at it knowing you can only please so many, and you've done all that you could.

The rewards are endless from pleasing people to the financial benefits. The sky's the limit. It truly is one of those jobs (like life) the more you put into it, the more you will receive. It can be very satisfying and humbling at the same time, or the same day, even within the hour. It's a job that constantly reminds you to stay on your toes. It is not a job for someone who doesn't put the time in, or doesn't plan ahead. It's also a job that is self-rewarding. Yes, you're selling a product or service that requires additional people to make happen, but it's YOU that starts this whole process.

38 Linda Pavlik, Regional Manager, Ember Farms

WHY I BELIEVE A CAREER IN SALES IS THE BEST JOB IN THE WORLD

Sales is a very exciting career for many reasons. When you think of it, we are all selling every day one way or another. We sell ourselves, we sell our beliefs, we sell our strengths, we sell our humanity. Sales is a wide open ~ the sky's the limit ~ opportunity that most careers simply do not offer!!! The very best reason to choose sales is you can re-invent yourself and apply some or all of your life skills to do so! Sales is and should be FUN! What career gives you the opportunity to reach for the stars and achieve your goals at the same time? A career in sales really is the best job in the world!

39 Steve Johns, President & CEO, More Online Profit

In my 25+ years in sales, I never had a job. Instead I chose to have a career!

Let me ask you a question, what other career allows you to help people save and make money, sell more of your product while letting you write your own paycheck? What other profession gives you the same feeling that you get after closing that big new account that you've been working on for months or years? There is NONE that compare to a career in sales!!!

40 Sue McConaghy, Sales Professional, Five Star Foods

"Every day is a great new day"............Our lives are surrounded by sales people, we are all salespeople in one way or the other. If you follow one rule: (A famous person spoke and his quote to this day is used over and over again: "Never give up, Never give up, Never give up")

41 Todd Richards, Sales Professional

WHY I BELIEVE A CAREER IN SALES IS THE BEST JOB IN THE WORLD

It is a job where the sky is the limit on your earnings as well as your own personal goals.

You have the freedom to own your own business but you do not have to inventory or warehouse any products yourself.

42 Steve Maiorano, Director of Sales, Landmark Foods

Bob here are some of the reasons I chose to work in sales 30 years ago. I sold the restaurant I owned and sill wanted to stay in the food business. I really did not want to work for an hourly wage being in business for my self. Food sales was a perfect fit for me. Being on commission, the harder I worked the more money I made. There was no limit to what I could earn. You can make more money in sales then many other professional careers. I worked like it was my own business. All the products in the ware house were mine all I had to do was go out and sell them. I didn't have to pay for them. I have a very rewarding career and still enjoy the challenges and changes that being in sales presents.

43 Libby Griner, Sales Manager

When you can fully stand behind the product or service you are selling it becomes your life. I stand behind my company's service 100%. I started my career in sales 9 years ago. I had never had any sales experience and I was scared to death. I mean the thought of actually going into a business and trying to sell something was a lot for me to overcome. Thank the Lord I did! I learned from the best. I would gather sales tips from this person and that person within my company.

The one tip that I will never forget is "N-O is nothing but a 2 letter word." Once I got the "hang" of selling it became addictive, and it still is. I actually enjoy hearing "no" several times before the sale. It makes it a challenge for me. Do I believe sales is the best job in the world? Well I can't speak for anyone else, but for me it is! I love motivating myself. There is no one in this world that can motivate you better than yourself! I love building relationships with clients, potential clients, and community leaders. Being able to say to yourself "This is what I want – and to actually go out and get it" is the best feeling in the world. I love setting goals and seeing my goals turn into clients. Then my clients turn into my friends. Then after enough time of 'taking care of this client" they become like your family. Being able to build them kind of relationships is more to me than just a job – it's my life!

44 Harold Price, Marketing Associate, Sysco Foodservice

First, I like how your statement is worded, "I BELIEVE a career in sales is the best job in the world.", Most people think or feel someway about something, they don't believe in what their doing is the best. If you don't have faith in yourself, the company you work for, or the products your selling, your success in the field of sales will be minimal at best.

Why I believe my career in sales is the best are as follows

1) You are out in the market every day, you see new people every day, and see first hand what is going on in your market, that way you can adjust tactics to help you reach goals set by your company and yourself.

2) Most sales people are paid on commission, you actually set your own pay, you are not restricted in what you make. Not many careers offer that way of making a living.

3) You can choose to work for a company that is number one in the products you are selling, first of all they want people that are excited in what they do, and usually your co-workers are firm believers in what they do also, surrounding yourself with a good company to work for and committed co-workers only helps you with your career, both offer good resources to help in your day to day work.

45 Mark Hallquist, Procter & Gamble Professional, North America Foodservice Sales Manager

Ironically, I had no plans to go into sales when I attended and graduated from college but I gave it a shot. When I started to work for P&G right out of college I opened up a new sales territory in Oregon, of all places. I was shocked with what I didn't know -- customers, products, pricing, credit, shipping and more were all foreign. My early days were tough. What I learned, however, was what a thrill it was to help customers solve their business concerns or issues through my solutions. I also learned that failure to sell a new idea or product happened on a regular basis. I carry that forward today -- sales is a series of highs and lows, and the highs far surpass the missed opportunities. Sales is a good career choice because you control your destiny more than you imagine and good sales people are a valued commodity in any organization.

46 Crystal Brown, Sales Manager

I love the diversity that I have in my sales career. Each customer is unique and complex in there own way. As a sales person we have to be all things to all people.

47 Ken Spurrier, Regional Manager

If you are one of those people who are content to go to work every day and do the same thing day in and day out, never experiencing the success that comes from a true accomplishment, then maybe sales isn't for you. However, if you know the rules and are **DRIVEN** to success, sales will give you what you are looking for.

The secret of success in a selling career is as near as your Collier's Dictionary...

D = Dedicated: To give or devote oneself entirely to some person or purpose. Working toward a shared goal.

R = Resource: That which is appealed to or made use of, as for aid or support. Skill and ingenuity in dealing with circumstances or events.

I = Information: Knowledge or facts acquired or derived as from study, instruction, or observation. Knowledge about a specific subject or situation utilizing data, facts and or intelligence.

V = Value: Relative or attributed worth, usefulness, importance or merit. Fair equivalent in money, goods, or services.

E = Energy: Capacity for, or tendency toward forceful action.

N = No: No is just a delayed Yes, the customer has just not figured that out yet.

48 Patsy "CiCi" Clements, Sales Manager

WHY I BELIEVE A CAREER IN SALES IS THE BEST JOB IN THE WORLD

Service, Service, Service…That's what makes a career in sales the best job in the world. Just think of how many different ways you can utilize "service" in you sales career. The first way is when you walk in your customer's door and instantly make them feel important. The greeting you use to start off this encounter. The enthusiasm in your voice and the SMILE (always remember to smile) on your face is the first impression you make with that customer. It spells "service." It lets them know that you are happy to present your product to them. It lets them know they are important to you.

Selling the "service" and servicing the "sale" is what make a career in sales so exciting. Meeting new people and getting to know them on a personal and professional basis only leads to the encouragement you need to make even more contacts. By interacting with them in conversation, lunches, phone calls, emails, notes and just a friendly wave on the street, you are selling and servicing that account. I want my customers to know that they get "me" in the package. I want them to know that I am "the service."

Nikos Kazantzakis, a Greek writer, once told Apolo Anton Ohno, the Gold Medalist ice skater, "We shouldn't be so concerned about winning or losing. What is important is to carry the struggle further." You will not win every customer and sell them

63

your product. However, what we learn from each customer's experience is important to remember so we can in-corporate it into our next sales encounter to further our sales career.

A career in sales offers you rewards. Not only are you meeting new people and making long-lasting friendships and partnerships, promoting your company which provides new exposure, offering a great product (that you truly believe in), you are also selling yourself. This alone gives you the opportunity to take pride in yourself, see your strengths, develop more confidence in yourself, strive to reach the goals you have set in your life and work harder every day to become the best salesperson you can be.

Why do I believe that a career in sales is the best job in the world? Because it will allow me to be more creative, to excel where only the sky is the limit, to become the person that I know is inside of me longing to be exposed to the world, to provide excellent service to other so they can also achieve their goals, to listen to what my customers are saying and continuously try and "think outside the box" in order to provide the excellent service that they deserve.

Why do I believe that a career in sales is the best job in the world? Because I believe in my company, my product, the service and myself.

49 Donnie Wade, VP Foodservice Sales, Atlanta Foods International

A career in sales is one of the few professions that give you the opportunity to earn what you are worth. Put a lot in - get a lot out. Be mediocre and make mediocre money. It is all up to you! There is nothing worse than sitting in an office on salary making the same amount as the person next to you and working twice as hard. Make your own future by choosing commission sales.

50 Molly Maynor, Sales Manager

I believe a career in sales is the best job in the world for one important reason - It lets you get out and meet people and learn the way life goes around.

51 Nolen Cleaves, Asst General Manager, Ben E Keith

I don't want you to go into sales! I want you to go and work in an office, punch a clock twice a day everyday for 3 or 5 years.

When you make the decision that you want to be your own boss, control your own destiny, then call me and let's talk about sales and why it is the best job in the world.

52 John Terpsma, Sales Professional, Lincoln Poultry

Hi Bob. Thank you for the Sales Course it really helped me focus on many of the aspects of selling. Now for the fun part of helping you with the sales speech. With a little help from famed sales trainer Zig Ziglar.

In sales you get to help people get what they want and in turn you get what you want. In sales you have a small but mighty part in helping this countries economy. By selling products and services you create demand and growth for the companies that you represent. People have work to do because you sold one Case and every case that is sold, needs one more case to be made to replace it ,thus helping our economy. In sales you have the opportunity to manage and grow your own business. In sales, once you are good at it, you'll never have to worry about finding a position in sales. There are thousands of products and services in which to sell.

53 Mike Press, Sales Professional, Banta Foods

Why would anyone want to have a career in rejection? Why would anyone go out day after day knowing that your pay is based on someone else having a good day. Why would anyone in the world work a day for someone else and not be paid for those efforts that day.

The answer I would, I do, and I love it. A career in sales with the correct training is real freedom. The benefits in a nut shell are, that for the most part I'm my own boss. My pay is directly related to my efforts. I schedule my day and meet who I want. I get satisfaction for a job well done all day long. I get asked all the time what's your future in sales and tell them what ever I want it to be.

No other job that I've come across gets my blood pumping as sales does for me day after day. It's not adrenalin like jumping from an airplane or driving a sports car. It's different, it's very powerful.

You feel as if you can do anything in the world. That first positive look from a prospect, or when you sign that first sales order, when that new client thanks you for your help, when you receive a commission because you know you did your best - that's a powerful feeling. And I can repeat it everyday of the week if I work at it.

54 Belinda Saville, Gearhouse, Sales Professional, South Africa

Thanks for your informative e-mails. Here's why I think sales is the best job in the world.

1) No cap on income potential, you can dictate your own salary
2) You meet many people from different walks of life, so it is never boring
3) You travel
4) You learn something new nearly everyday
5) Your hours are your own
6) It's fun!

55 Josh Gordon, Account Manager, Banta Foods Inc

We are the quarter back of a team. We are the ones that make changes in the plays/sales that not only make our customer/guest of our company happy but also the company. We are the decision makers of our company and our future. There are some people that can crunch numbers, there are people that can read people to hire, and there are collectors, but we are people who can do all. And we are salesmen.

Regardless where I am at, I am the face of my company. I act not only as Josh Gordon when I walk, but I represent Banta Foods Inc.

56 Al Hitch, Commercial Sales Manager, Gordon Food Service

Most of the time I don't even think of this as a job in "sales". I look at my job as an opportunity to help my customer achieve their goals. If I can do that, then I am successful. I enjoy using all the tools available to me to help my customer. It really motivates me to know that I have helped my customer with a menu or brought some ideas to them that will help put money in their pocket. Of course, when that happens I usually get an increase in my paycheck as well. I also enjoy the contentious learning that takes place in our industry with all the new products and changes that take place.

57 Cullin Hamm, Branch Manager, Ambassador

A job in sales is truly the best job anyone can have. If you believe in the product or service you are selling you are essentially trying to help you client. It is the best feeling in the world to know that you have helped one of your clients. Another great aspect of sales is that you are control you own destiny. Most people in sales work on commission or at least a percentage of the profit. The better job you do, the better reward you will receive.

58 Paulette Clarke, Ambassador Personnel

Sales opens a world of knowledge unlike any other job. It offers flexibility, creativity, unlimited potential in terms of earning power, as well as ability cross social/economic lines by meeting people from every walk of life. The benefits are enormous if you are energetic, motivated, and can work independently. The same conscientious, driven effort required to graduate from university, applied to sales, can guarantee your success.

59 Brian Dubin, Branch Manager, Ambassador

1- You have the freedom to chase the accounts you want to chase

2- You can make your own schedule, to some extent.

3- You have certain freedoms on a daily basis. You can penetrate an account from many angles. You can pick & choose how to proceed.

4- You can sell in the industry for which you have a passion.

5- You can ride-with vendors to effect sales.

6- You can ride-with in-house specialists to effect sales.

7- You have the freedom to be yourself, and not just be the corporate stuffed shirt.

8- You meet people.

9- You can primarily follow-up and chase those that you like.

60 Stacy Jefferson, Regional Vice President, Ambassador

I worked in construction during summer breaks for several years while attending college. It was the greatest job. I was excited every morning about getting to work. The reason is you can see your results! I view sales the same way. There is nothing better than making a quality sale and seeing the results. The results are a happy customer, a bigger commission check, and in my industry, a happy employee.

Another reason is earning potential. A true sales position allows an individual to earn as much as they want or can. I worked in the banking industry for six years. My salary was all I could earn. My current position allows me to earn a salary and bonus based on profit and production. Therefore, every day is an opportunity to increase my income.

61 Robert Prickett, Director of Sales and Marketing

Why I believe a career in sales is the best job in the world...

1. Income. If you are NOT motivated by earning enough money to enjoy a great lifestyle, then selling might not be for you. However, if you enjoy being financially rewarded for your effort, there is no better career than sales.

2. Flexibility. There is a freedom that comes with sales that very few other careers enjoy. This can be a double edged sword. Some people can't function when they are in complete control of their day. If you have the discipline to make a daily plan and stick to it - sales is where you belong.

3. A noble profession that fills the needs of others. If you are in sales with the attitude of "what's in it for me?" I predict failure. However, when you focus on giving extraordinary service to your customers, sales will reward you.

62 Todd Hauser, AFDR President (Ten Million Sales Pro, Martin Brothers)

Being in a sales job can be one of the most fulfilling jobs if you are set-up to be a sales person. The Sales Person's set-up is like this:

Curious, friendly, outgoing, competitive, caring, high-strung, problem solver, knowing a little about lots of things, etc --is a good make-up for a sales person. Not everybody is cut out for a sales job, so identifying what your make-up is sometime in the next ten years or so should help you figure out if a sales career makes sense for you. Even if you find yourself in a sales job and you don't feel like you're really cut out for sales, you can still be successful if you follow some basic principles of sales--like, do what you say your going to do, be truthful, always be a professional, treat your customers and the company you work for the same way that you would want to be treated.....If you do these basic principles, I BELIEVE A CAREER IN SALES IS THE BEST JOB IN THE WORLD ::))

63 Gary Sanchez, Sales Professional

Success is a blend of Vision, Faith, Confidence, Patience, Planning, Knowledge, Commitment, Desire, Responsibility, Passion, Courage, Momentum, Persistence and a clear understanding as to why we want what we want. A career in sales is not for the faint of heart, clearly the breakthrough of overcoming those intangible mental hindrances that limit our ability can only be achieved by facing the humbling truths of our innermost being. Inspire yourself with a desirable purpose, conquer your fears and aspire to the challenging yourself daily. The results will take you where few will ever go. Experience lasting success.

64 Barb Ward, Sales Professional, Troyer Foods

Why Sales is the best job in the world!!!

I sell FOOD: To groceries, to restaurants, to caterers!
I have daily goals: Fill my trucks, Sell more than any one else.
Help the customer with new items.
Always try for one more case of product per order.
Get the most products out my customer's door!!!
Teamwork, Teamwork, Teamwork!

My rewards are fantastic, not just monetary...
"The item you recommended is great."
"Send me another, Thanks for recommending that."
"What else is good?"
"Thanks for helping my business grow."
Where else is the job satisfaction so high?

Besides that, I love Contests!!!!!!!!!

Sales; of any sort is a competition. I like to win!!!

65 Steve Morello, Facciola Foodservice

Growing up I enjoyed playing competitive sports. Anticipating, planning and practicing for the Game. I love the high victory brings and also how to deal with defeat. Even today i play golf and shooting my best round gives that same feeling. When i have a bad day i try to figure out what was wrong so next outing will bring better results. Working in sales closely resembles playing sports. You have an objective account you are going after. Find out everything you can about that account. Put together how you can win the customer over and execute your plan. When you get the account there is that same feeling of great satisfaction. By chance after all your planning you are not successful, learn from the experience so you can get better results on your next objective account.

66 Rodolfo Yanez (comment - here's a story you HAVE to read)

WHY I BELIEVE A CAREER IN SALES IS THE BEST JOB IN THE WORLD

When I came to this country I couldn't understand a word in English. I could not communicate at all, other than in my own language - Spanish. I worked in different jobs from dishwasher to clean up person for a huge food processing plant while I started taking ESL (English as a second language) classes. I had a strong desire to continue my education; however, my work schedule conflicted so badly with school schedule that I had to quit either my job or my school.

At that point, I decided to do two things: First, to find a job that would let me keep on going to school. Second, not even thinking about quitting my school. I could not find a job. Therefore, I decided to get into sales - by necessity not by choice.

It turned out that being unable to find a job was the best thing that could ever happen to me. I had an old computer and bought cheap design software. I spent long hours figuring how to make it work. When I mastered a few tricks to enter text and import clip art, (please note that this is something that third grader can do) I visited 20 different business in the area where I used to live. I collected their business cards and asked them how much they had paid for them, took them home and spent about a day working on five of those business cards. Next I visited different printers in the area and I found one that was a "wholesale printer." At that point I didn't even know what it meant, but I found that their price perfectly fit into what I was looking for -a little bit more than half of what those business owners had paid for . The next day I went back to those businesses and I told them that I could print their business cards for less and have them look much better than what they had. I collected 5-7 orders that day and 5 the next day and that was the beginning of...the whole enchilada!

I have spent long hours reading about the principles of selling, and once you get into sales you have to get into marketing, psychology, negotiation skills and many other areas. It is exciting!

Thanks to "SALES" I was able to negotiate with my teachers - when I was unable to turn in my projects on time! Because of the SALES job I chose when I could not find anything else I was able to finish my education and start my own business! I became so good at what I was doing that after I graduated from school I decided to work only a brief period of time - two years- and then moved into sales.

Because of the SALES I became self employed; opened my first cell phone store and did great. I opened the second and the same thing happened. January of 2006 I decided to get into something new. The restaurant business and it has been the knowledge I have about Sales what have let me keep my doors open! and it will be the same concept what will keep me going...and going...and going... I still have a long way to learn and do more than what I have done so far.

SALES instill in you traits that otherwise are much more complex to acquire. The reason is simple you experience them by doing them, by acting...For example there is no way to be in SALES and have a negative attitude. Sales make you think of yourself as a winner not as a failure. In sports, the star team members think of themselves as "winners" in SALES...sales professionals think just the same way.

Am I bragging about myself?? Not at all. I am bragging about SALES...SALES...SALES...AND MORE SALES just because a career in sales is the best job in the world. I can go to Chicago, Mexico, Argentina, China, Europe, all over...apply the same principles and make a decent living...and that's what matters! I have not found any other career that gives you the same benefits whatsoever!! Try and see for yourself...

67 Jeff Tieger, Sales Professional, Facciola Meat Company

1) You are your own boss

2) The income potential is great

3) Get to meet a huge number of great people

4) You get tangible results and praise for your individual effort- not a "cog in the wheel."

5) Sales is a constant learning experience.

6) The travel is great

68 Anette Booth, Sales Professional, Saval Foods

What better job can you have to help people get the best product for there money and to also help them learn how to set it to their customers. Plus, make money for the customer while doing it. Who could ask for more?

69 Karl Hansen, Director of Marketing, John Morrell Foodservice

Freedom, Independence, Different, Educational, Discovery, Problem Solving, Rewarding, Personal Growth and Life Changing. These are the words I would use to state why a Sales Career is all about.

The **Freedom** to create your own success.

The **independence** to work the way you think.

Different, you make a difference and each day is different in challenges and scope.

The career is **educational**. You learn everyday. You get to discover new things about people, places and things.

Problem solving is what you really get to do. Finding out how to solve problems and find solutions. Rewarding, is a great word to talk about sales. It is a great feeling to help people solve their problems and help them. By being a sales professional you **grow as a person** everyday with learning, insight and new experiences.

Finally, sales is **life changing**. You change your life and the people you interact with in doing what you do every day.

What other profession provides freedom, education, reward and discovery while giving you personal growth, problem solving and the ability to change your life?

70 Jeff Sigal, Regional Sales Manager, Ember Farms

It is the best job because every single aspect of one's life is dominated by sales whether an individual knows it or not. When you wake up in the morning to the minute you go to bed, you are actively participating in the results of the sales process. By participating in sales, you get to improve the lives of people on an everyday basis.

71 Eric English, Sales Professional

I love sales because I am the master of my own destiny, I pretty much make up my own hours, control my income and sell mostly to people I like selling to.

72 Giselle Hudson, Trinidad

I must admit: I didn't find sales, sales found me. Jaded from my University experience, and my own "young at heart-foolish" choices I landed a job writing up delivery notes for a packaging company. At that time I thought that "there must be more to life for someone who "almost got their University Degree" and although the memories are vague I believe that I asked my Managing Director if I could fill a position in the Marketing department. From my view out in the heat, close to the factory, the Marketing job offered the perks of air-conditioning and being able to visit the company cafeteria and maybe just maybe get to drive a nice car. I know, back then I was pretty "deep". I had no idea who marketing was or what he was about but I was about to "do marketing" and boy was I unprepared! My sales manager gave me a list of names and sent me out on the field. Yes - no preparation - just the names. I can't say that I was a good salesperson or a bad one because I got paid regardless but this would be the most valuable foundation laid out for me in the world of business.

It has taken about twenty something odd years - but finding and keeping a job in sales has molded me into the person I am today. The person who loves who she is and loves what she is doing. This is not an egotistical "Oh I'm so in love with myself" deal but one of hope for anyone out there who has ever had the thought that they were less than others and not amounting to much.

Sales has taught me discipline. I have learned that there are no short cuts in life. I certainly tried to bend that principle and break it in two and every single time I did something "half-way" the results were quite painful. I have learnt responsibility for self and for my results. I think that I made a huge breakthrough when I finally understood that I was the reason I was where I was. Once I took responsibility for my low or no sales things started to improve. Along the way I made a little money, and I made a lot of money - none of which I was keeping. Staying in sales taught me that it's no fun making money when you can't keep any of it. If you want to know how to suck the joy and life out of any sales person it's to give her a bonus and a stack of bills simultaneously! Even though she's happy for her reward she knows that she has just enough to cover her expenses. That sucks!

Selling kept me picking myself back up and trying once again. At times it feels as if you're wrestling a monster and then there are those moments when you feel at peace and at ease. I learned that I needed to stay in the game.

Finally, I think I've come to the point where I know what I want and have to do in life. I have discovered my purpose. A job in sales, allowed me the time to discover, and learn things about myself that no other job could match. A job in sales has given me moments of reflection - those dark lonely and sometimes sad moments, where you want to give up, give in, and throw in the towel - but you know deep down that you just can't leave because sales is your way of life. It is now a part of you and you could NEVER EVER divorce yourself from it - even if you tried -

even with the pain. Because you understand that the world moves because of sales. Nothing happens without sales. We all sell every single day of our lives!

 When I look back over the years, I've made many many friends. I have seen mother's give birth, I've celebrated many birthdays and promotions and I've seen some folks pass on but their collective memories will live with me forever and that my friends is priceless. Now I know that being in the sales profession is the best University degree that I could ever have pursued because not only did I learn different techniques and skills but I learned about life! And for that I will be eternally grateful.

 My name is Giselle - and I'm proud to be a sales person!

73 Kristine A. Sexter, Senior Consultant, Speaker & Trainer

There is no career better suited to today's modern 'overachiever' than sales!

1. Sales is ideal for those that value relationships. Even in the face of modern technology, that continues to literally separate us from our customers, the best salespersons intimately identify with the needs of their customers.

2. A sales profession is the finest example of "work/life" balance in today's existence! Think of it this way- Don't work/ don't produce results (also know as - sales!)= no money. No money? Well- no life. No life? No 'balance' to be concerned about!

3. I know that the America's Ivory League schools will soon offer a 4 year degreed program in sales because it combines all the disciplines of:
a. Psychology (relationship development)
b. Technology (keeping in touch)
c. Accounting and Finance (If you're good- you'll need the accounting and finance acumen to invest all the money you'll be making!)

74 Amy Grimm, Sales Professional

I am a divorced mother of 3 young children. It is Halloween night and each of my children has Halloween plans. Therefore, I am able to catch up on some of my paperwork while they are out with their friends. However, if my children needed me to take them out for the evening I would have been able to do so and get caught up later tonight. The FLEXIBILITY allowed in this profession is PRICELESS.

This is not to say that sacrifices aren't made. I attend chef's association meetings & local restaurant association events a couple evenings a month. I feel like my family life and career balance well, all because of my career in SALES.

75 Jeff Bruce, Sales Manager, Northern Haserot Brandt

Bob, here is my list in no certain order....sales is a career that I thought was a business of "untruthful" people...instead I found the most driven, thoughtful, engaged, honest, & committed individuals that I like to call friends, confidants, cohorts, and professionals. You, yourself have proven that sales is a very rewarding career not only financially but spiritually. Let's not forget that sales is a profession in which you develop some of the most spirited relationships you will ever find. Finally, I like to say that there are two kinds of individuals who work for any business....those who consume "cash" and those who produce "cash"....I like to say that the **sales people** that I have grown to know...**produce** "cash" for their organization!!!! Thanks for allowing me to participate in this exercise.

1) If you want to rely on no one else but yourself, choose sales
2) If you are 100% totally committed to the task at hand, choose sales
3) If you are goal oriented, and it "turns you on" to reach for the goal, choose sales
4) If you believe in holding yourself accountable, choose sales
5) If you want control over your personal income, choose sales
6) If you want to look forward to a career in which your daily career life changes, choose sales
7) If you want to run your own business, but don't want to assume the risk, choose sales
8) If you truly believe that nothing gets done with out a sale, choose sales

9) If someone told you that you cannot do something and you want to prove them wrong, choose sales

10) If you want to go to go to sleep every night knowing no one controlled your destiny but YOU, choose sales

11) Lastly, if you think you have the gift of gab and can "fool" everyone...PLEASE DO NOT CHOOSE SALES!!!

76 David Kubisch, Regional VP/Sales, Performance Food Group

Now, for the endorsement of the sales career. I can tell already that this will be way too much—please feel free to edit, excerpt or totally disregard (I'm a tad passionate about this topic):

A) Own Your Own Business with ZERO investment

~~You don't have to purchase any inventory

~~No mortgaging your life savings (or your wife and kids)

~~No imploring "Friends & Family" for financial help

~~No personal risk or indemnification

~~No spoilage or lack of movement concerns

~~No creditors knocking at your door

~~No tort-happy lawyers looking for your head on a platter

B) No need to purchase/lease warehouse space, materials handling equipment or staff, delivery trucks/drivers, office staff, etc.

~~No Government oversight

~~Federal, State and/or Local Taxes & Regulations/Inspections

~~No Payroll to meet every week--with the EXCEPTION OF YOUR OWN!!!

~~You don't even have to buy or maintain your own computer, etc.

C) No A/R to carry or A/P to manage

~~No staff to hire or train and manage (see above)

~~You only have to manage your personal expenses and communicate with your clients about keeping their bills paid

D) Be Your Own Boss

~~Set your own schedule

~~Within reason, especially if you are dedicated to your own personal development and improvement

~~Set your own goals

~~How much do you want to earn?

~~What will you sell?

~~To whom?

~~Devise your strategies

~~Learn as fast as you can and develop your skill set

~~You can even chose whom you will service and work with

~~You just have to Plan Your Work & Work Your Plan

~~You DO have to get yourself out of bed everyday, get yourself prepared and go to work--and BRING YOUR BRAIN WITH YOU!!!

~~Take advantage of a FREE Support Staff

~~DSM and Specialists

~~Advice and training

~~Professional support in closing deals/sales

~~Technical support & Product Knowledge

~~Department Heads and contacts

~~Customer Service and Delivery Drivers

~~Brokers and Manufacturers Reps

E) Positively impact the world and make it a better place

~~Help people solve their problems

~~Deliver results that make a difference

~~For your customers

~~For your community and its institutions

~~For your Company and teammates

~~For yourself and your loved ones

~~Fulfill needs and earn the right to satisfy your own

~~Ala Stephen Covey: to live, learn, love and leave a legacy

~~Become a resource to yourself and those around you

~~Build this business of yours with a soul and a conscience

~~Recognize, develop and deliver on your best instincts

~~Focus your integrity and your efforts on improving yourself and your world

77 Betsy Thomas, Regional Sales Manager, Ember Farms

"Why I Believe a Career in Sales is the Best Job in the World."

What other career gives you the opportunity to meet & interact on a daily basis with people from all walks of life? It also gives you the satisfaction of helping someone improve their business or organization because of the product or service you can offer. A commission sales career can also give you an opportunity to earn more income than a career in another field with a set salary.

78 Dick Alexander, Professional Speaker and Consultant

Why I Believe a Career in Sales is the Best Job in the World

Before I begin this article I want to make a distinction between a salesperson and a clerk.

When I began my career (over thirty years ago) my first sales trainer was the owner of the company I worked for. The very first bit of training I received from him was a very clear and distinct lesson on the difference between a salesperson and a clerk. A clerk, he said, was merely an order taker. They added nothing to the buying process. A salesperson is an individual that acts as an advisor. They know (and understand) their product and/or service as well as the competitions product and or service. They know the strength and weaknesses, as well as features and benefits of their products and/or service as well as that of the competition. They know and understand the wants and needs of the customer as well as the wants and needs of the company they work for.

My memory of that lesson stops there. As my career progressed I have added to this lesson. Just knowing and understanding the items above is not enough. What I think needs to be said out loud (that I think my boss assumed) is all of that information needs to be translated into value for the customer. So in my mind I am a value translator. Very few people, in my experience, whether it's the people who design the products or deliver the service, speak the language of value. Value is a language all to it's self, and very few people speak it well. Those who do...have the opportunity to make more money than those who don't and deserve to live better than those who can't.

In addition to having the opportunity to make more money and live better, I like being in the position of making a difference. A company can have the best product or service in the world but until somebody buys it, it's worthless. Salespeople make the difference. Very rarely if ever do we get the opportunity to represent the best product or service in the world, but the dynamic is still the same. Sales makes the difference. And in my mind it's a critical difference with a delicate balance.

The balance is what I call the value triangle. Imagine a triangle, at one point is you, another point is the company, and the last point is the customer. The balance loosely goes something like this. I need to sell enough goods and services to satisfy my basic wants and needs, plus satisfy my goals for a better life for me and mine. The company needs you to sell enough goods and services so that it can make a profit and grow. And the customer needs value and a relationship with a trusted company and company representative that make their life better. If anybody in the triangle gets greedy (out of balance), I don't get what I want and need, the company doesn't get what it wants and needs, or the customer doesn't get what they want and need, commerce stops and life is harder for all involved.

Personally, I like being in a position that's critical to the company and valuable to the customer. Like the saying goes "it doesn't get any better than this."

79 Ron Sonedecker, Division Trainer, US Foodservice/Cleveland

Although someone could write a book about "Why I feel a career in sales is the best job in the world" I am going to highlight why I believe it to be so. My career spans 20 years in sales and am currently a corporate trainer in sales and leadership.

A Sales career offers the right person the following:

The ability to control your income...More productive effort relates to more income The ability to continue to grow in your skills to adapt to the ever changing environment You are never as good as you can be and are constantly honing those habits and traits that made you successful You must enjoy the challenge that there are always other sales people trying to take your business. If you are not competitive by nature don't chose sales as a career. The highs of winning are great but ability to come back from defeat is essential. You must be a people person and realize there are different sales techniques needed for different customers with specific personality traits.

The most essential sales trait needed is the right communication in the right format to the right person. You can look in the mirror each morning and be talking to the CEO (that is you) and determine how successful your company (sales results for that day) is going to be. You control your Attitude "Attitudes are Caught not Taught" If you have a bad attitude it will be perceived by everyone you come in contact with that day. You have the ability to make it a great day.

80 Mark Koschny, Sales Professional, Lee Foodservice

Selling is an entrepreneur's dream job! The sales rep is really an independent contractor / consultant (not just to the prospect) but to the employer. The sales rep's asset is time...the amount of time and the quality on how the rep deploys his / her time results in increasing levels of compensation.

81 Gary Holbrook, Sales Manager, Brown Foodservcie

"Why I Believe a Career in Sales is the Best Job in the World."

Top 3 Reasons:

Write your own pay check every day

Not have to do the same thing two days in a row

No one to answer to but yourself.

82 Austin Smith, Branch Manager, Smith Family Foods

I believe a career in sales in the best job in the world because of the longevity of partnerships/friendships you create in your business world. Also a great arena to showcase how devoted you are to your career and company. As for me, our family business survives on sales alone, if we're not out there selling, we're not providing for our family.

83 Lee A. Dec, Sales Professional, Saval Foods

Sales is the best job in America. Where else can you use your knowledge and people skills to make money? People skills are very easy to learn but hard to master. Let your client talk, not you. Most sales calls are killed by the sales rep talking to much and not listening to find a need. The beauty of this is if you learn to listen and understand what the client has a need for so you can sell them. We have raised the bar as an industry. People are now looking to there Sales Rep for answers. Only those rep's who chose to take it to the next level will succeed If you can solve problems and like the ever changing daily challenges of sales. This is the best job in the world. You are your own boss, within a company structure, you meet or exceed your budget and you are a hero. And finally, this is your business to run. If you do well, this is your company to run as long as you choose. What other job can you find that has this to offer.

84 Wendy Parrot, STOP Restaurant Supply, Canada

Why would you choose a career in sales? Simply put flexibility, the challenge and the ability to be in charge of your on destiny (pay cheque).

Section 2 Staying Motivated

I received over 70 replies, from highly successful and motivated sales professionals, to this question:

"How I Stayed Motivated After the Initial Enthusiasm

Wore Off and the Reality of a Sales Job Set In."

I am sure you will agree, after you read their words of wisdom and advice, this will be, without a doubt, the best book on sales motivation you have ever read! Why? Because it is all based on the real life experience of successful people who are LIVING IT EVERY DAY. There is no fluff. No hot air. No trying to impress an audience. Just real, honest-to-goodness sincere answers to a question given in the spirit of helping a friend.

01 Bob Oros

In asking myself what keeps me motivated the answer is simple.

Why do I send out 400 sales letters every week?

Why do I write at least one article every week?

Why do I email a selling tip to thousands of sales people every week?

Why do I get up at 5:00 AM and answer 50 to 100 emails?

Why do I travel over 100,000 miles every year?

Why do I call 25 to 50 people every week?

Why do I give seminars to thousands of sales people every year?

Because there is NOTHING more rewarding and motivating than to know that I am helping someone become more successful. Helping someone increase their business. Helping someone make more money. When someone calls and invites me to speak at their sales meeting, or someone orders one of my books or enrolls in my sales course, or someone signs up for my selling "newsletter" it just doesn't get any better than that. When you really understand that SERVICE IS THE SECRET OF SUCCESS YOU NEVER HAVE TO WORRY ABOUT BEING MOTIVATED – YOU ONLY HAVE TO WORRY ABOUT FINDING ENOUGH HOURS IN THE DAY TO GET EVERYTHING DONE THAT YOU WANT TO DO.

02 Brian J. Hopkins

Here are my thoughts and ways that I have been able to maintain my motivation over the years.

Here are the things that I did as a sales rep to be successful and what kept me motivated. They are simple things done over and over again.

1   Set goals that are not easily achieved and review them weekly.

2.   Do sales calls that are repetitive - constant practice is what makes perfection.

3.   Have some fear of failure - fear of failure is a great motivator.

4.   Build friendships with customers and they will expect you to be at their place of business regularly.

5.   Read about successful people and imagine what it would be like if you were that person.

6.   Learn about the most successful person in your company and work on becoming that person every single day.

7.   Motivate yourself by setting a weekly and monthly schedule and don't let yourself get drawn into jobs that are not beneficial to your goals.

8.   Work for a company that has goals and desires that mirror your own.

9.   Have an Ego.........it will make you want to win.

10. If you are a territory rep make sure you start everyday early and focus on seeing customers early......the early bird get the worm.

11. Plan your work and then work your plan............it will keep you focused and make you work even when you feel like taking a day off.

12. Have a mentor and talk to that person as often as possible.

13. Focus on what it takes to make the income you want and what you have to do to achieve it and work it everyday.

14. Do your job; think like you own the company and you'll never get bored.

15. Know your business and make each department know you care about their success.

16. Communication of challenges and successes.

17. Be motivated and positive in everything you do and it will show to your internal and external customers.

I hope this helps Bob. Thanks,

Brian J. Hopkins, Vice President of Sales & Marketing

Flanagan Foodservice

03 Troy Deag, Australia

Well Bob, there is no secret as you know. The only solution is to reach deep inside oneself and create that enthusiasm. That's it; it is and always has been an intangible concept, enthusiasm. Because of this, an enlightened person has the ability to create it themselves. Now there are a myriad of ways to create this and I recommend a self study course or a mentor that will literally kick you up the ass when needed....

Oh, there is one more way...SELL MORE. It's self-perpetuating.

Now, excuse me but I believe you have taken me away from my primary task of selling...

04 Cyndi Maxey, CSP

I remember clearly. I wouldn't stop between phone calls. I wouldn't even put the receiver down. If I kept at it, I would get an appointment. I would envision the appointment turning into a trip to San Francisco which was my first big trip. I would think. One of those names on the list will turn into a really neat job - like the one in San Francisco that I envision!

P.S. And just last week I watched in Pursuit of Happiness, and guess what? The main character did the same thing with the phone.

Cyndi Maxey, CSP, President

Maxey Creative Inc.

05 Nigel Boswell

Keep setting targets and achieving them - sales, profitability, new accounts.

Keep learning new sales techniques. Keep learning about the business I work for and how it works. Keep learning about the products I'm selling.

Become the "expert" in categories

Keep learning more about my customers business so I can help them more in unique ways

Nigel Boswell, New Zealand

06 Jeff Lydeen

I turned my sales goals into their monetary equivalent and put my dreams into writing along with pictures of them. I was no longer trying to hit a number or quota but rather trying to obtain the object I desired.

P.S. It helps to date a "high maintenance Blonde"

07 Bob Mackie

Points to make:

Your personality must be challenge driven.

You need to be a PHD: Poor, Hungry, Driven.

You've got to be excited about helping customers.

Set levels of goals: account, route day, week, month, year.

Discuss with senior reps in the company.

Sometimes taking a day off and totally focus on what you are doing and what you "need" to be doing on your route. Long and Short term.

08 David Cobb

You stay motivated by having fun! If you have fun, it will take the drudgery out of sales and you will be successful. If you are having a good time then it will rub off on your prospects and it will be reflected in your sales.

09 Shannon Gross

I feel that we all at one time or another fall into a rut. The best way that I like to stay motivated is to spend time with my family. I have a beautiful wife, and a nine-year old beautiful daughter who both want certain things. Please notice I said they have wants, and not needs. I think that a sales rep in a rut can provide needs for his family. However, the wants cost a lot more than the needs. The wants will require that me as a commissioned sales rep do certain things. My daughter wanted a trampoline at the beginning of the spring. I was able to provide this want because of staying on top of the game. When my wife or daughter asks for something, I hate to say I cannot afford it. If I do have to say that, then I make a point on Monday morning to excel at my job as a commissioned sales rep with no cap. My point being, that I can control my income. My father's favorite quote is, "if money won't motivate you, then nothing will". I enjoy my job, but I do not think that I would do it for free. I have worked for other food companies in the past. I have never had the support and continued enthusiasm from management that I currently have with Roma. Robert Prickett is by far the best manager I have had. I am sure you have noticed his enthusiasm with his job. He takes it very seriously, and the enthusiasm rubs off on the entire sales team. I do not know who said this, but it is a great quote. "Attitude is a reflection of leadership". Would you not agree?

10 Joyce Stallard

Well Bob, It's like this. The initial enthusiasm wares off occasionally but not for long. In other words, it's kind of like taking a slight nose dive and then heading straight back up. I know it is normal to get tired sometimes but if you are a true bred sales person, you will never give up. The reality of a sales job can be difficult on a new sales representative but should be expected by an experienced sales person.

The excitement of helping your customer and knowing he or she is happy generates self motivation. Making friends and keeping them is a great thing! I love all of my customers no matter what. You can't win them all but your attitude can help you win most of them. Wake up with a positive attitude; work hard, take care of your customers and the rewards can be outstanding in every way!!!

11 Scott Caldwell

How I stay motivated is simple. I pray every morning that God will be with me and that I will have favor with my existing customers and prospects as well. Every day offers new opportunities and challenges I am committed because my family is counting on me to provide for their needs. My customers are also counting on me to be the very best I can be for them too. I truly Love being in Sales, most days that is.

12 Mauricio

I stay motivated by focusing on the upside of getting the account. I think about how many opportunities I will have to show them how to increase their sales or save money. I am also motivated by having an opportunity to show what our company has to offer. My motivation is determined by how much I can help the customer and if I do my job correctly, my personal and financial payoff will be met down the road.

13 Mike Dosset

I like people and being able to help them be successful in making money. I will be able to accomplish my goal by helping my customers get to their goals. By asking and listening to what they are trying to get done.

Knowing whom to get the help in getting them where they want, and what they are looking for.

14 John Waugh

Here is how I would approach it right or wrong: First of all they have chosen their profession and if they want to be a DSR why not be the best? I always compare business to being in sports; do you want to be a mediocre player with a mediocre salary or do you want to be a star with a great income? I think it comes down to the individual because successful DSR's are the one who are self-motivated day in and day out and if they don't have those characteristics then maybe they should find a different career. I have found over the years that the successful ones always seem to find a way to get back to the top even if they loose a big account and that goes back to self-motivation to be a winner and always having a plan. Another analogy I use is marriage.

Even after the honeymoon is over you still have to find ways to keep the relationship fresh which goes back to being committed to the relationship. These are just a few of my thoughts and I hope they help.

15 John Feri

I would stay motivated after the initial enthusiasm and the reality of a sales job set in by staying focused on the skills and strategies I have learned through my training. I take pride in doing a good job, so self satisfaction and company recognition drive me. The compensation that comes with selling might motivate me a little bit as well!!

Thank you,

John Feri

Marketing Associate

Sysco Food Services

16 Roland Degregorio

As you may know, I have been a restaurant operator all my life and this is the first time being on the other 'side of the fence'. Like the tides in the ocean, there have been many ebb and flows. I have realized the harder I work, the high tide stays longer. The happier I make a customer, the high tide stays longer. When I make a sale, the high tide stays longer. When my fellow associates and my managers recognize my good work, the high tide stays MUCH longer. It is these ongoing thoughts of success that gets me through the low tide. I also realize I have a way to go to get where I want to be. I just have to work harder on getting a bigger boat. In addition, I sometimes feel I am a better teacher /coach /manager than a sales person. Example: I am lousy in golf, but can easily help/teach others improve their game with tips and training I have learned. I just can't help myself to lower my score. It is easier to teach than learn.

Finally, when I joined the sales team, I had all of these ideas of the 'low hanging fruit' of customers I already had a relationship with in our industry. I now realize the fruit is there, but much higher in the tree than I thought.

Hope this helps.... Roland Degregorio

17 Jeffrey Sherman

Motivation can vary from person to person; one person might see a goal of a new car as motivation to do well. Another might do best with some ongoing external inspiration. For me as a business owner, going to seminars tends to fire me up and get me wanting to improve my business. While "out of the office" events can certainly be best (particularly when there are great speakers), sometimes just an hour-long online webinar can do the trick.

Jeffrey Sherman

Warever Computing, Inc.

18 Lewis Hoffman

Goals. I don't mean company goals like monthly or annual quota or x amount of sales calls to get a prospect or a sale. I mean personal goals. It is very simple. If I just focus on selling $110,000 per month then it can be frustrating on days that I get beat up and lose a sale or don't achieve an advance in a sale etc. etc. Indeed call reluctance can set in.

But....if I focus on my personal goals: Providing for my family. Keeping my three kids active in sports. Being top sales representative in my region. Increasing my commissions 15% so I can put money away for college.

These personal goals drive me to go on to the next sales call. These goals overpower frustration and call reluctance and keep me from sitting at Sonic shuffling papers and drinking cherry limeades. If I am touch with what is really important to me then it drives me to action.

I also believe that a sales manager needs to get some idea of the personal goals of his sales reps so he can motivate them toward those goals and not just a company quota. I have sat in cars with reps ready to quit but if you help them focus on why they got into commission sales and how it can help them meet their personal goals then that is much more motivating than talking about things like getting a no puts you closer to a yes or other standard sales speak.

19 Jordan de la Morandiere

Selling is like a game, we always strive to win. Some games we win, some we lose, but it is the feeling of getting that win that keeps me going. Granted, the initial enthusiasm does wear off, but it is the anticipation of that next big win that keeps the fires burning.

20 Thomas R Cosentino

That is an outstanding question. I believe the key has to be self discipline. It seems that we are spending more time chasing the dream rather than applying the principles taught us. Almost as if we are searching for the easy answer rather than working through the process to reach the desire goals.

Thomas R. Cosentino
Performance Food Group, Mutli Unit Manager

21 Laura Czajka

Well Bob, I don't know about you, but each time I make a sale, or place a candidate at a new client, I get that little butterfly of excitement. I am still young, but I think 20 years from now, I will still get that same feeling when I do something successful. The thrill of the chase is what keeps a lot of people going. Some people are addicted to gambling, or drugs, but I truly enjoy the feeling of having a goal, striving to achieve it, and then succeeding. Another huge motivation to do well is the fact that this is my career, not a hobby. If I want to make money to do the things I want to do, I HAVE to do well. It isn't an option!

Laura J. Czajka, Staffing Specialist, Ambassador

22 Rick Hughes

The way that I've stayed motivated has been more a pride thing than anything else. I really don't enjoy being at the bottom of sales reports, contests, etc. and I feel a little embarrassed whenever I do occasionally end up there. On the other hand, I really do enjoy all the rewards that go along with being towards the top of the sales list. Although we all work for money, that's certainly not the only thing that motivates me and apparently others. (look at any pro athlete that signs a huge contract; 99% of the time they have a sub par year right after they get more money.) My boss is very generous with other motivating factors, such as trips (and time off for said trips), prizes, and bonuses. All of these things along with a little intestinal fortitude have kept me going long after the new wore off. Thanks,

23 Jennifer Kendrick

Great question! I'd tell the audience that the initial enthusiasm we all feel as a sales person is only the foundation to building a successful career. Once the "newness" wears off it is imperative to stay focused on the big picture and the end results for each sales call. It is important to know that we will not close every call, however we can learn from every call we make and if we take those lessons and apply them to the next call we are sure to be successful. When we get discouraged then it is time to "think out of the box" and dig down into out creative side to plan a new agenda. A sales person must assess their performance on a daily basis and focus on what we did today to get us to the next step of closing a call. Setting daily, weekly, monthly and annual goals and most importantly knowing how you plan to attain those goals will help keep you focused on the big picture. SMILE! Before you walk into your office every morning SMILE! Before you walk into each sales call SMILE! Always remember to "SMILE & MEAN IT"!

This is just the tip of the ice burg and I could go on an on an on.....Receiving these motivational emails enlightens my days! Thanks,

24 Donnie Wade

Actually, I have an answer that would work for this that I emailed my sales team this morning. Taking things for granted. Ever here that phrase? It is a big part of everyone's life everyday. We all take things for granted on some level every day whether we intend to or not. We do it at work and we do it at home.

When sales are sluggish, like they are right now, it is a perfect time to take this phrase to heart. I would like for everyone to step back today and think in terms of NOT taking anything for granted with your customers.

Assume that you have to start all over and earn every case that they order. If you don't take anything for granted in each and every customer you will see a sales increase, you will feel better and your customers will feel better about their relationship with you. They will see that you appreciate their business and that you are enthusiastic about helping them manage their business.

So, go out there today and start all over. Ask every customer if everything is going well, what can we improve on, are there new products that they are looking for, can I bring by some of the new 2000 items that we inherited from CMC, are our trucks making deliveries on time, are our driver's courteous, what else can I do to assist you with your business, how else can I earn more of your business, invite them to the golf tournament, etc.

25 Otis Boyd

Corporate Vice President, Ambassador - Bob: I am motivated from with-in. I already know that I cannot service all the business out their so, when someone says no to me concerning a sell its ok. I want to do business with the people that want to do business with me. Also, I work for myself and my family and if I cannot stay motivated I am not the man that my father raised. I also learned the best time to make a call is right after I closed a deal because my confidence is at its peak. A salesman requires a lot of rest to be at his best. So to be at my best I need to have a good plan for the day, week and month and well rested. Whistle when you walk. It makes a difference. In closing my job is to motivate me not you.

26 Theresa Pritchett

After 9 years of Recruiting, I still get excited and motivated about my job. What I have learned over the years is you have to search out, initiate, and make connections to keep yourself motivated and enthusiastic. For me personally, relationship building with my client's always excites me. Yes, we are in sales positions, but ultimately, you have to make connections, earn trust from your client's and listen to their needs. This is the challenge.

27 Wayne Gauldin

My wife Betty is a DSR (Sales Associate) for GFS and she was a DM 10 years for TPC, I do have a great "resource" for helping you here.

That reality sets in FAST. Early failures kill enthusiasm. I would open my speech by quoting an old proverb, Success breeds success.

Everything that you and I have always taught should be brought into this one.

Such as

1. Be yourself

2 Plan your work, work your plan...

3 In that vein, be a list maker

4 Be a master at follow up

5 Don't be afraid to make cold calls

6 Do those extra things for customers they never expect.....gifts, cards, on appropriate occasions

7. Learn the art of increasing order size....suggestive selling. KNOW when the competition has stolen an item away

8. Know where you stand...am I primary supplier? Do I have 50% 80%?

9 Don't rush through the sales call...don't let the customer think you need to be on your way.. He is KING (a GFS-ism) Make customer know you CARE

10 Don't let credit issues kill the relationship

Bob I can go on and on here, but I am not sure I am taking you where YOU want to go with this. If the rep plays the game straight and is always honest and dependable, customer will fall in love with him or her.. and when we are loved we can hold on the that enthusiasm. I see Betty woo accounts and they LOVE her because she is on time, truthful, goes the "extra mile".....you know all that stuff.

Let the customer down, get "sloppy," and the customer starts to react....or go away.. so therein comes friction...friction kills enthusiasm. Does any of this help?

28 Mike Melton

I like to think that I am service oriented and fairly organized. My main thoughts would be to stay organized with the onslaught of incoming customer needs, focus as much as possible on customer needs, and seek new opportunities. I also feel it it very important to know as much as possible my competitors strengths and weaknesses. If a customer tells me in conversation that one of my competitors is weak in an area I began to work on that area for the customer. If I could sum it up, I would see what my customers needs are, focus on them, build confidence in my abilities with my customers, and continue to work to know where my competitors are in their plans. Continuous successes and enthusiasm will automatically follow.

29 Alex McQueen

After the wedding and the honeymoon ....real life sets in and you need to maintain the passion , the drive and the BELIEF ....REAL BELIEF that you are going to make it. I received this at our trade show on Tuesday Bob and while my mind was occupied with other things I started to think about the answer.

Being a meat guy I like to trim the fat and get into the meat of the matter as quickly as possible so my answer is simple, in fact I would like to sum it up in a phrase .

THE WILL TO SUCCEED!

With out this nothing will work. Goals / Planning / Follow up / the list goes on.

That is my simple answer Bob from a simple guy.

I am a great student of history Bob because history give us an understanding to our future!

We just celebrated the 90th anniversary of an important part of history in Canada "Vimy Ridge" How did the Canadians in WW 1 achieve this victory after the French , British and Americans tried to take the ridge. From what I have read the Canadians had huge losses yet they were victorious. Was there will greater that the other, Simply put Yes

Same thing for the shores of Normandy in WW 2 . The planning was there, every detail was worked out apparently but when the proverbial @#$% hit the fan all bets were off, yet despite HEAVY losses and a unfortunate underdog position on the " low ground " on the beach the Allies were victorious....why? The will to succeed on the Allies side was indeed greater than the German's

Bob I do not know what your views on the Vietnam conflict are but I grew up in that period and I also am very interested in that era. How could the most powerful nation on earth not succeed? Trust me Bob I am not trying to be smart here or insult anyone. I know there are many factors in that conflict but the will to succeed with a belief in the cause and conviction to act, I feel was greater with the North Vietnamese that with the US .

What motivated the people ...fear maybe ...I believe that fear can motivate like money can motivate, it is a temporary motivator. The real motivator is one's conviction to the cause.

Sorry for the long explanation for a " short " phrase answer but the power of the human spirit and what it can achieve is the most powerful force in the universe if the will to succeed is present.

30 Craig Culbreth

How many of you in this room are in a rut...You thought that the job you were in was the best thing ever you busted your tail, and now you show up to work or go on calls like you are going through the motions. Well I'm here to tell you that starting tomorrow you are going to be a better salesman just because you walked in this room. It is hard to believe isn't it. It's quite possible that most of you are thinking that this is officially a hoax and you are ready to leave, but let me tell you why your not. Your not because you want to make more money. Your not because you know there is something better out there and an opportunity to get a little insight on how to get it might just be worth your time.

That's right gentlemen and ladies, you started a job that you "thought" you could make a lot of money in and you jumped all into it and after awhile things might not have been working out, or you did not like it so much anymore, who knows? You know a lot of people have the same reaction to things they do in life. They are ready to turn over a new leaf, they dive into it head first they start seeing a little change or some results and they become satisfied and quit. Are you satisfied with what your doing. Its okay if you are a good life can be lead with just being satisfied with what's going on at work and in your life. You can have a family and a house and car and go play golf on Sundays with being satisfied.

I look at a lot of you in this room and I have to tell you Satisfied is just not on most of your minds. It is time for a reevaluation of what is going on with you from the inside before you can go and fix what's wrong on the out. Sure this job was great at first and you might have kicked but at first but what now? Well I'm here to tell you I'm not satisfied. I never have been and I never will be. That's just me...I want the green pastures and I want it to be a lot greener in my wallet is well but that can not be done by being satisfied. Don't get me wrong there will be no effort without short coming, but you have to make a decision, am I going to approach my job with a new vengeance. Let me give you some advice to...Let them know. Tell your boss or your manager, listen I have been satisfies with what I'm doing but I'm not satisfied with being satisfied any longer. You pay attention to what I'm doing, I'm going to take care of my end of the deal and I expect that will take care of yours. Now what manager is going to argue with that? And don't do it alone, tell your other salesmen, lead by example. Ladies and Gentlemen success will only be gained by those that have the correct interpretation of what success is. Its........whatever you want it to be.

31 Nolen Cleaves

In sales the enthusiasm should never ware off, if it does then you need to look for something else to do. If you ever look at sales has a job then your not in sales. Sales are not for everyone but if you want to have full control of your income and working day then sales is for you. Now lots of peoples will say they want that control but are not prepared to do the things day in and day out to make it happen. My Uncle was in real estate sales for 30 years and he gave me his personal quote when I got into sales. He said live by this and you will have much success and when you stop doing this, then it is time to get out. I had this taped to the back of my front door so I would see it everyday when I left my apartment. "Out work'em, Out sell'em"

32 Scott Heatherington

What would I say to a group when covering the topic "How do I stay motivated after the initial enthusiasm wares off and the reality of a sales job sets in"?

I would start with a buy in question to involve the group and to set up the topic, something like; "How many of you have dragged down by the relentless battle of sales"? Obviously, the entire group would raise their hand. After making them "sick", I would make them "better". "How many of you want a new perspective"? I would expect that the entire group would again raise their hand. This type of intro sets up the idea of something new and creates an interest with the group.

My topics would then cover the Idea of Choice, Time management, The Thrill of Competition and finally Taking Action.

Everyday we wake up and put one foot and then the other on the ground. At that point, it is a fresh NEW day. Your choice is to decide if it's going to be a good one or a bad one. I would then continue with the process of positive thinking and effective planning.

That would dovetail into some time management skills. There are 86,400 seconds in a day. We must plan them and use them effectively. If we don't use our time, others will. There is a thought that work expands to fit the time allotted. We need to plan work and time effectively.

I would then continue with the flexibility that a sales position offers, the opportunity to create a New Day every day. I would talk about the "Thrill of the hunt" that skill set that takes us from a cold call to a close. I would focus on the excitement and adrenaline rush that occurs when we bag that new account or get that sale. It makes your heart pump and your blood pressure soar. (In a good way)

Then I would talk about the money. As I have often told my sales people, "your pay raise becomes effective when you do". If you want to make more money, go and earn it. That is the excitement and enthusiasm in our business.

I would close, as I often do, with a challenge to take action. Nothing changes until something is done. There are 3 frogs sitting on a log. One decides to jump off. How many frogs are left? Well, there are still three frogs. Deciding to do something is not taking action and doing it. Until one of those frogs actually jumps, the answer is still 3. So, go and do something.

That is a few thoughts on how I would handle it. I hope it helps…really.

33 Morgan Frazier

The thrill an excitement that awaits is very motivating. When you have gotten to the point where you can look back and say oh yeah all that hard work has finally paid off.

34 Steve Dirks

Simple - the power of written goals, reviewed 3 times daily and read out loud to myself. My mission was/is to make a mark for myself and a life for my family

35 David Kubisch

Aside from just being a "Foodie" and loving the Industry, the way I stay motivated is by fulfilling both Personal and Professional needs:

1) personally, I love to "Win" (maybe I am motivated by a fear of failure?), so staying current, educated on trends and product knowledge, refining communication/sales skills, etc., means "never having to say you're sorry" by giving me an edge over my competition and dis-information;

2) professionally, I get a lot of satisfaction from solving my customers' problems and helping them be successful (in spite of themselves!), "earning the right" to the annuity that is their continued confidence and business.

The only difference between obstacles and stepping stones is the attitude that you take to them--my job is never boring or routine, every day presents a new challenge, and I feel blessed and lucky at the same time. Besides, feeding America is a worthy calling!!

Best wishes, and thanks for your support,

David Kubisch

Regional VP/Sales

Performance Food Group

36 Bob Beasley

I stayed motivated by actually making the sale! I can distinctly remember the rush I would get when a customer would really let me work for him. By that I mean to use what I knew to recommend the best for him and I could sell it at a fair profit for my company. Great feeling and the only way to get it was to be successful in selling. I learned more about selling and my product on my own than company sponsored training sessions.

Bob Beasley, Fadler Foods

37 Lori Randall (2005 Mrs. Christian World)

I kept myself motivated by reading stories of others who had overcome the obstacles and made it in sales.

I kept myself motivated by surrounding myself with encouraging people who believe in my abilities more than I do.

I tell myself over and over...I am filling a need. I am providing a service, product whatever that will change their lives.

Finally, I look at my bank account and am scared to death! Yes, sometimes fear moves me off dead center.

Hope these help.

Lori Randall

38 Ron Fenton

It's all about attitude!

39 Cliff Potts

I have never been one to read about motivation! I believe that most of us stay motivated for some of the same reasons. Wanting the best for our families helps us to stay motivated is one!

There are times when it is hard to stay motivated. When there is for every 40 cold calls to potential clients you will receive 2job orders for example.

I try not to look at them as turndowns but as learning experiences to apply with the potential client next door. I know there are a lot of things that motivate me! Some of them are very small day to day experiences.

Personally when you work on a client and you finally land a big job order! Seeing a team come together to do everything that it takes to fill that order. Then there is the excitement of accomplishment throughout the office!

I ENJOY BEING A PART OF A GROWING OFFICE!

I also find motivation in helping people. A few weeks ago an employee of ours that went full time came up to me thanking me for giving him a chance at a job!

40 Kirk Purnell

Good sales people are never satisfied and have a passion for constant improvement. You can always do better and should always be looking to learn more to add value for your customers. Kick yourself in the butt so you never develop a comfort zone or an attitude where you aren't seeking to learn and get better.

41 Carrie Smith

The more I learn about my product and the way it improves the lives of the user really fuels my passion for what I sell. When I'm passionate about what I'm selling, it's easier to engage the potential client – they want what I've got. I learned that once I asked enough questions to find out what their needs (and pains) were, I could better tell them what they needed to know about my product. There's just something about being interested in a client's needs that engages them in the sales process. It makes my job much easier.

42 Jamie Register

I communicate with peers to perhaps swap stories of success. Those that have far more experience than I, without knowing it, keep me motivated because I am competitive by nature and want to always be on top just as they are. Then there is the mental game where you have to realize that not everyone will buy the first time you talk to them. In fact, it will take 5 or more calls before you close. I take a step back and reflect on what I have learned from both training and my own experiences. I always, always, always try to stay away from negative people. They will drain your energy within minutes.

43 Lynn Good

I will keep this short. To keep me motivated I think back to all my customers that have thanked me and have told others about how much I have help them with ideas and service. Thinking about that helps me remember that, if I can get the customer to open up to me, I can help them. Knowing I have something to offer the customer, other than just taking an order, makes my job much more interesting and rewarding.

44 Kyle Eastham

Hi Bob, Here are my thoughts...

Remember why you took the job:

1. Was it to get experience in a different field? (that exp. will come day by day)

2. Make more money?

3. Change of boss?

4. Better working conditions?

5. To get a full time job at that company? (in the case of a staffing agency)

Whatever the reason, keep that reason in mind. Write it on the bathroom mirror, on the sun visor in the car, wherever you'll see it several times a day.

To excel, be willing to give 1-3% more than everyone else. Kentucky Derby winners, NASCAR drivers, and Olympic swimmers win by fractions of a second. Their margin of victory is usually less than 1% better than 2nd place and no more than 3% better than the rest of the field. Yet they get paid 5, 8, or 10 times more than the rest of the field.

That means staying 15 minutes later, making 1-2 more calls than everyone else, hand-written thank you notes, literally smiling when you talk on the phone, and giving people a little something extra (a free sample with their regular order, a $5 gift card to Starbucks, sending a Halloween card (everyone sends

160

Christmas cards), or something else free or inexpensive to set you apart.)

Those cumulative efforts, over time, will result in better relationships with customers, more sales, higher sales, more repeat sales, and a higher salary and promotion for you!

45 Vern Holder (Professional Speaker)

I have some basic things that I use in Sales.

1. I don't sell anything, I solve problems. By keeping that in mind I really feel I'm helping my customer. I try to find out as much as I can about my customer so I can imagine how my helping him/her will affect his company, family etc.

Sometimes, I tell my customer, "I don't sell anything, I solve problems. If I can't help you I have no business being in your office. And likewise, my company expects me to sell something sooner or later! But I've found that if I help solve a problem, sales take care of themselves."

2. There is nothing as great as a customer telling you of a problem and you have the exact perfect product to solve that problem! Sometimes I customer may not know he has a problem or there are new products on the market that will him be more efficient, and thus more successful. And it is your duty to tell him how your company can really help him.

3. I've never been mad at a customer. I've been disappointed that I did't get the order, But the customer has the right to say "no". But a "no" doesn't mean I've lost the order, it only means I'm not finished yet! I ask questions and then try another sales technique.

4. I've used this technique for years. By keeping track of how many sales calls I make a day and my sales for a year. I divide my yearly sales by the number of sales calls I made that year, I know that each sales call is worth maybe $500. Suppose, I find I

must make 10 sales calls to get one $5000 order. Then I physic my self when I get a "no" I tell myself, (thanks for the $500 order!) This keeps me motivated and upbeat all day long. Sooner or later that $5000 order comes along. Or maybe I get three $5000 orders in a row. Wow, that's when I go fishing!!! Bob, this might sound goofy but it has helped keep be "up" and motivated during all of my sales career. It works for me. By the way my largest single sales was 1.1 million and we were not the low bid! I fished for a week!

46 Sue McConaghy

Continuing to learn the business,

Asking questions,

Listening to their needs (customers),

Creating a need/want.

Sampling products.

The key is don't become stagnant. Enjoy every day, smile, have fun and become important/valuable to your customers.

47 Kristi Pinckney

Two ways:

First the success of others keeps me motivated due to my competitive nature. If they are doing it then so can I and better.

Second keeping updated on new products and training techniques keeps me motivated

Territory Manager US Foodservice-Salem Division

48 Otera Sanford

Always have a POSITIVE attitude! Customers like a positive happy person to brighten their day! It makes them feel good and that makes me feel good; even if the last call or previous day was not as profitable as I had anticipated. Look for some new challenge to overcome. Stubborn customer or prospect just will not cooperate! Use feel, felt, found, and testimonial letter and prove other customers do like me and my company. Also, read one of my testimonial letters. Reminisce about a great sale or comment from a happy customer! I like ME; I am a good person; and I want to leave a happy thought to brighten someone's day!

49 Tom Pangburn

I would review my goals (which I have written down and look over regularly) and chart my course against them... that gets me back on task every time.

50 Jon Mangiaracina

If you are out there making enough calls and really doing your job then the job will stay fun and motivating. The more calls I make the greater my opportunity to make the sale and there is nothing better than that feeling of closing the deal. By making more calls you increase your odds of success.

Jon Mangiaracina, , Escalon - HJ Heinz

51 Vickie Anderson (Professional Speaker)

For me, it's about all the things you've taught us. I realize that it's a lot about timing. Just because someone doesn't need me today doesn't mean they will never need me. If they meet the profile of people who could use my services, I just need to keep in touch with them so they will think of me when their need arises. Also, I really like your idea about I need to qualify them to see if I want to work with them. I have control over who I do business with. And, finally, I like to think to that I have useful information for people, so why would I withhold that from them? It's my duty to offer it to people to see if they could use it.

52 John Carter

One of the things I encourage our sales team to do is to set goals and keep them in front of them where they can constantly see them (dashboard of the car for example). It may not even be the written goal, but what that person will benefit from hitting the goal. For example, if a person has a goal of making enough spiff for a cruise, having a picture of the cruise ship plastered where you constantly see it helps keep the eye on the ball and provides constant focus.

53 JoAnne Welch

I would say that any job in today's society is a lot of work. We all have bad days from time to time - but it's by looking toward the future as to where you want to go and not focusing on where you have been and what you have done. Keeping your goals in sight and working on them, and modifying them as time passes will help to keep up your momentum to sell, and keep you in a positive frame of mind.

With applying fresh new ideas and concepts to the negotiation with your accounts or the portfolio of accounts that you manage will help to keep the relationship evolving. Being their partner in business rather than looking them as the customer that's going to pinch pennies with you this week. It's all the perspective in which you view the customer. We are in control of how we feel and how we interact with others.

54 Chadney Sawyer

"How I Stayed Motivated After the Initial Enthusiasm Wore Off and the Reality of a Sales Job Set In."

Attack each account (old) as if it were a new one. Remember that we are in the business of creating revenue and giving people security in their jobs. We hold the livelihood of others in our hands and we should be happy that we are making such a difference in so many people's lives.

What other job can you meet and influence so many people and help businesses grow. We have the pleasure of making businesses profitable and we make a difference every time we sell product to the customers! That is something we can be proud of. I get a great sense of enjoyment in going home to my wife and telling that I made a difference today.

Be proud of what you do! Chadney E. Sawyer Food Service of America

55 Jeff Ramesbottom

My motivation comes from excitement I get from working with my customers to solve their problems. Having them see positive results from the fruits of my efforts replaces the thrill of a single sale. Oddly enough, they seem to buy more when I am not trying to just sell them something.

56 Teddy Bazakos

We are in an interesting arena, the sales arena. For me personally, motivation comes as we face new challenges, new competition and new friendships'. We are in a field where most of our clients and customers become our friends. We have the opportunity to make way for new friendships' and solidify old ones. To wake up everyday and to be in a position to help someone's business to be more successful and to help with his bottom line is a great feeling. When we go out of our way to make something happen and the customer appreciates our effort to help his business he doesn't need to say "thank you" the inner satisfaction is enough for us.

To be able to imitate that feeling day after day provides me the motivation needed to service my accounts, represent my company in the best possible way and to make a few good friends along the way.

57 Ric Newell

Always do the hardest things first. If I do the worst thing first
then even difficult jobs seem a little easier. It's kind of a mind
game but it keeps me on task. I work from home and am my own
boss so staying motivated can be a problem this little exercise
assures my cats have a clean litter box and my worst job is over
as soon as I get out of bed.

58 Joy Christopher

I am a Marketing Associate for SYSCO Foodservices of Alaska. I stay motivated by reading materials, videos and cds on selling. I also look for unusual food items to show my customers and this helps me to get excited all over again. I also talk with my fellow associates, "pick their brains" and share my experiences. I love my job, have been in sales since 1994. In the foodservice industry you can never say I have nothing to do. I love food magazines, shows, internet websites etc. I try to find new and exciting things for my customers. They look to me for ideas and I love it. I'm a foodie. I just ordered a sample of alligator sausage for some of my customers to try, how cool is that. This job is never boring, very competitive and frustrating, never boring!!! Sysco has an amazing array of items and services to offer our customers and it is my job to use all the tools to make my customers money and in turn I will make money. I'll admit my blood is SYSCO blue, I'm a Sysco blueblood!!! You have to enjoy Your job and when you begin to dislike going to work, its time to evaluate what you are doing. Sales are the lifeblood of society, tough, but rewarding job. I originally became a sales person because your success depends on what you put into it, not if your friends with the manager. I worked in Restaurant management for the government before sales.

59 Mark Koschny

I make an effort to look at sales as a contest... understanding the prospects psyche, buying motivation, pain, opportunity, asking questions that drive to the personal impact of buying or not buying. If I can qualify a buy / no buy I have won...better to have a yes than a no; better to have a no than a maybe

60 Sandra McMaster

I would say you are selling the wrong thing... or need better understanding of what you are selling. I sell well and easily motivated when I'm helping people get what they want and need... finding it... understanding it... overcoming their resistance to helping themselves... etc. But have the believe in and understand the product(s). From the heart. If in your heart, never problem with motivation. If having a tough day... smile at first customer, ask them how they are or what exciting thing they did so far today... and when they smile back, I'm ready to go.
Sandra McMaster

61 Ed Noe

Bob---for me, the answer is not a "one size fits all" and assuming that I still believe in the company I am working for or the General I am following...then it comes down to my competitiveness and conscientiousness. Personally, I have been able to stay positive knowing that I have done a good job even if the accolades or sales results are not immediately forth coming.

62 Craig Osmond

Motivation comes from the desire to want more, why do we work? We work to live and to achieve more. We do this by making more money and to get more money the company must do two things, (1) gain more sales (2) get more margin to get the profit needed to pay more. One is no good with out the other, so we learn and teach more to stay ahead off our competitor so we can get these goals.

When a coyote gets up in the morning he must run faster than the slowest deer to eat and survive. And when the deer gets up he must faster than the fastest coyote to survive. So no matter were you are on the food chain when you wake up you better be running!

63 Tony Watson

People motivate me and I know in sales that I will be dealing with different people daily. Problems and opportunities will present themselves each day as well. The way we handle those problems or opportunities will determine our success with that client long term. After twenty years in foodservice sales I am still presented with the chance to learn something new everyday as well.

64 Crystal Brown

The easiest way for me to stay motivated is to celebrate every success no matter how small it may seem. We receive a lot of No's in our industry. It would be easy to get frustrated if you did not focus on the Yes's or even the Maybe's.

65 Heidi Wilson

Sales will always have highs and lows. Always! In our industry you have to remember the "Big Picture", which is to connect people with job opportunities they may not have had before. Some it is a chance to start a career. Others it is a chance to gain a good income. Some may even increase their current income!

Everything that goes down must come up! With sales you may need to "regroup". Look at your sales approaches and if you can make changes. Always freshen your approach. It keeps you, the salesperson, going and upbeat. It works for me!

66 Lynn Mosely

Let's see, what motivates me? Well, a good nights sleep is one thing. I can't get any sleep if I did not do my best during the day. I was always taught that any job worth doing was worth doing well. That is how I approach my day. I need to be proud of myself and the work that I do. It represents who I am. How I feel about myself matters most, however, I want to do a good job for my company too!

I enjoy the material rewards of working hard. I am a single income family so it all falls on me. If I don't bring it home, no one does. I know this answer is boring, but it is the truth. I guess I could say something like "World peace depends on the job I do!" Not so much……

67 Robert Prickett

Because in my job, my customers are the sales people in our organization, staying motivated at all times requires little, if any, additional thought beyond the knowledge that 25 people, each and every day, depend upon me to get things done so that they can make a living. It is, I believe, similar to what one feels in the process of child rearing.

Sorry to be so short in response, but if I carried on further, I'd start writing that book I always said I would write my very best to you............ and yes, the "really" is what get's it done.

68 Bill Adams

Being in sales I have had the opportunity to listen to or read material from a number of Professionals whose living depends on motivating other people. Sometimes I was forced to, sometimes I went for the entertainment and sometimes I paid out of my own pocket because it was and investment in my future. I'm sure you know which ones I got the most out of, you're right, the one I made a personal investment in.

For me to make the investment I first needed to learn about the speaker, what do the have to say that could benefit me (WIIFM)- What's In It For Me). Get my self excited about going to listen and learn from this person. Take notes during the event If I felt the bond I would buy the books and CD's offered at all of these events.

Set my SMART short term, intermediate and Long Term Goals.

Every week, every day look at my goals, review my results and measure my progress. I know I will fall of the wagon, I don't look at that as a failure, it is what it is, I just fell of the wagon. I review why I set these goals, I revisit my notes and material that always tells me why I committed to change. I may not always reach every goal but I have always benefited from this process.

How to you maintain the enthusiasm after reality sets in.
In Short, enthusiasm is a living thing-it has to be feed and watered regularly or it will die.

69 Tom Wheat

I stay motivated by the dynamics of food service sales. It is always changing. Food service is not static. Customers, vendors and products all change. I enjoy the challenges of continuous organizing the purchase and sales of products.

Tom Wheat

70 Tim Krueger

I think the biggest de-motivator is hearing no over and over again. I just view this as a set back and tell myself that next time thy will say yes because now might just not be the right time, I never take no personally. In my life I know that there are times when things are tough and I have to say no so I figure soon I might be able to say yes so why not for others to. I always say thank you whether or not they purchase from me. I also give them a card and tell them if they should change their mind or if there needs should change to let me know because I would like the opportunity to serve them. I also ask if they would mind if I checked back in the future. Most of the time I leave with a good feeling. I also tell myself if it was easy everyone would be selling something and would be rich. Just put it into perspective, look at a baseball player's batting average, they don't get a hit every time and they sure don't hit a homer every time. Thanks,

71 Wendy Parrott

How do you stick to anything that is worth while. Simply put, I feel if anything is worth doing, its worth doing well. You may not always be able to stay on track but what is important is to try and try again. You will get there. The road won't be straight as there are always going to be interruptions and you may have to side step a time or two, but you will get there. They tell I'm tenacious, so I guess that helps!

72 Michael Murphy

You need to keep your spirits up. Every day is a great day some are just more challenging than others.

This job will throw many more defeats that wins. You have to focus on the wins and block out the defeats. This is not to say don't examine the defeats to learn what you could do better or different.

Your motivation to stay in this Professional Sales position is the paycheck at the end of the week. The solid relationships you build. The satisfaction of helping someone else make money and succeed.

73 Kristine Sexter

Here's how I motivate myself and the metaphor I often spoke of when I worked for Robert Half International which required each inside sales persons to make 100 sales calls per day- football!

"Motivating yourself to sell each day is like playing in the Super Bowl. Every morning you must rise with a bright outlook upon your abilities, remain faithful in your Coach's resourcefulness and insights, and remember the unwavering need your current customers and future customers have in your product or service.

You were picked for this team because someone saw, and deeply believed, in your talent. If your past performances have affirmed your greatness, then know that it still lives within and may just need a new approach to reawaken it. This is where you can utilize the skills of your Coach! Your Coach may not have ever been a star player, but they too have been chosen because of their unique ability to motivate and direct. In a true sales environment, your Coach may be your manager, your mentor, a colleague, a parent or even an author.

And don't forget those Superbowl commercials! They are the most coveted advertising slots and certainly the most expensive on TV today! Why? Because millions are watching! The sales process is alot like these commercials- are you broadcasting your message in a manner that develops a relationship with a buyer? Do people remember you long after you are gone? Are you, as a salesperson, as reliable and consistent as the "commercial" you project to viewers/buyer? And are you broadcasting it enough to actually get it to stick in the minds of those that watch or are they tuning you out?

Suit up! Lean on your team and coach in times of disappointment but never stop playing- especially when you know, in the deepest parts of your mind that you care about those you serve- your customers... your fans! "

74 John Storm

As far as my answer to the "What keeps me motivated after the initial enthusiasm wore off of a sales job" question, here goes:

I spent over a decade in the sales world, specifically consumer products in the sporting goods industry. My responsibilities ranged from managing a global sales force to personal responsibility for national accounts like Wal-Mart, Kmart and Bass Pro Shops. There were several things I used to keep me movitated over the years:

1. Lifelong Learning: I constantly looked for new ways to improve and be a lifelong learner. I enjoyed reading books outside my field, looking for applications to my sales responsibilities. I bought audio tapes to feed my mind. I went to seminars to grow my skills. I interviewed all different kinds of people and tried to find out what motivates people to buy. Sometimes, I'd turn the sales challenges into a game, trying to find as many new angles, spins, pitches, and approaches as I could. The key was to not get stuck in doing things the way I'd always done them before.

2. The 3 C's: Much of my motivation came from what I call the 3 C's: Colleagues, Customers, and Competitors.

Colleagues: We had some fantastic sales reps who were full of both wisdom and experience. I loved to find out what other people were doing and then try to twist, spin, and/or modify their techniques into something I can use to differentiate our products in the marketplace. My co-workers were also extremely bright and talented so I continually learned from them.

Customers: I was fortunate to have some great customers who understood and valued the word "collaboration". I constantly learned from them - what worked, what didn't, and benefitted from developing personal relationships with them.

Competitors: I had a healthy respect for our competitors and tried to learn from their successes. Knowing they wanted to take away my business was always a good source of motivation too!

3. Values: It always helped to remind myself WHY I did what I did. I had a family depending on me, as well as my colleagues and other company employees. I didn't want to let them down. One of my favorite Bible verses says "Whatever you do, do your work heartily, as for the Lord and not for men." This was a reminder that my work mattered to God and that I should work "heartily" for my real "Boss". Plus, I desired to be a good steward of the opportunities that came my way. So, overcoming the temptation to quit, or settle for something less than my best, required me to focus on the bottom line values that drove my life and work. Some days I succeeded and some days I failed ... all part of the learning process that still drives my life today.

75 Cee Coats

Everyone starts a new job with lots of enthusiasm. Everything is new and exciting. But, over time, you find out all of the not-so-nice things. Starting at 7: 00 in the morning and still working at 10:00 at night; all of those customers that have had a bad experience with your company in the past; that sales manager that was so kind in the beginning know doesn't care to hear anything but how you plan to make your numbers for the month; etc.

There are times that I have started to work in the morning and by 10:00am, I'm thinking I should have stayed in the bed! I have found the best way to handle that is to go back to bed! Really! On those days, and they are rare, I go back home! I spend the day cleaning my office, throwing out all of the junk I don't need anymore, organizing my files, and calling my special friends and customers that always seem to make me feel better. By the end of the day, I'm good!

Everyone needs time to chill. Time to think about what you (used to) love about your job, what you dislike about it, and what's changed. More times than not, I find that what has changed is me! I get down over what a coworker said. Or maybe it was that big account that fell through the cracks. Could be that the elastic is too shot in my panty hose! Who knows? One thing that works wonders is going to my "mentors". I read once that we should all have mentors. Make a list of quotes made by people you admire. These are your mentors. Refer to them when you need that extra push. My all time favorite was said by Thomas Edison. During his quest to invent the light bulb, his assistant asked him, "Why do you keep trying? You have failed over 5000 times." Edison replied," I do not know failure...I have discovered over 5000 things that don't work." Failure is the major enthusiasm killer. No one wants to fail. But it's not a failure if you learn something. Now, when I walk away from a prospect without the sale, I just tell myself...Okay, that didn't work. I take notes, put a smile on my face and move on. It's what Dad used to refer to as a "bought" lesson! Life is short. Love what you do, or do something else!

76 Dr Burt Smith

Staying motivated in sales is no easy task. You are always looking for things that can be reflected upon to get a boost of motivation. Sales can also be a trying, even a lonely journey. Even if you're the president of the company, like I am, and I get to call myself the "owner," ultimately I'm still the sales guy.

What I use to help me stay motivated in the selling process is to remember that the main reason I love selling is that you have full responsibility for your destiny! You even have a degree of control over it. It can be the last hour of the last day of the last quarter of the year and if your numbers aren't where you want them, you can pick up the phone and make a call or send an e-mail or go knock on a door or do SOMETHING to create the destiny you want rather than feel stuck in the situation you're currently in. The ability to sell, to influence, to passionately solve others' problems is a very powerful thing, and showcasing it that way is very motivational!

Because sales gives us control over our destiny, I have always looked at my business as a way to give me the life I want, and as business planning, sales goals, service practices, or whatever, as the means to that end. I look at my life and my business as a way of life and try to imagine myself in a movie I'd make about my life. That can help make the hard times and disappointments a little easier to bear if only because it makes it a better story! Who would want to see a movie where the hero wins all the time? Great stories involve great triumphs over adversity! Losing a key sale or suffering disappointments make the story that much more involving! Not to mention how much we can learn from the good times and especially the bad. In sales, it's your destiny, your choice, and your story! You're the writer, director, and star of your own story!

Speaking of stories, here's one I'll defy any salesperson who deserves to be a member of this profession to see and not be ready to make a cold call after the credits roll! The movie is called *Door to Door*. In it Bill Macy plays a young man who has cerebral palsy and takes a job in sales. The sales manager initially turns him down because of his physical appearance but agrees to give him his worst territory. The entire movie is a great tribute to the human spirit and a reminder of the role sales professionals play in the lives of the customers we serve.

www.ingramcontent.com/pod-product-compliance
Lightning Source LLC
Chambersburg PA
CBHW032004170526
45157CB00002B/541